FREE FROM THE RUT

Reclaiming your Power

Jennifer Lynch

Sept 25

Dedications

To my sister Susan with love
Thanks for the happy times
Thinking of you, as I write this in
Your birthday month of June

And for Gay Harrison who brought so much
wisdom to my life.

For Dot Cooper who taught me joy.

And for Detta Darnell for your generosity,
spirituality and contagious laughter.

You will always be in by heart, soul sisters.

ABOUT THE AUTHOR

Jennifer Lynch lives in Norfolk. She's a keen walker, animal lover, and dancer. She started writing to keep her busy in the evenings when she was a single parent and didn't have a life! She now works as an empowerment coach and reiki healer, writer, and poet. Her books include The Silver Lining, William's Wishes, Liberty Angel, Never to be Told, Salsa, We Hear You Angels, 5th Dimensional Earth, and eBooks Shades of Kefalonia (meditations for the chakras) and Attracting What You Really Want.

She can be contacted by emailing
jenniferlych7@gmail.com
Or by visiting her Facebook pages
Jennifer Anne Lynch or jenniferlynchauthor
Instagram @jenniferlynchauthor
and Twitter @angelbrightness.

Please feel free to contact her for feedback or coaching sessions.

SWITCHED OFF

Georgia turned her mobile off in disbelief. Was Stewie for real? He couldn't see her for another three weeks. How could he expect her to wait that long, and more to the point, after this, did she want to? Their relationship had faced many challenges from the start, yet they also shared some wonderful times together, and now it had come to this! Did he even care about her, or was she being strung along? 'He'd pencil her in for next month' was the pits when she could so easily be rubbed out before they got there. How could this be love when it was obvious that she was number two in his life?

'Can't he ever put me first,' Georgia shouted angrily, as she slammed down her mobile phone.

The sensible side of her said, 'You allowed this, in fact, you encouraged it. You felt flattered by this man because you craved attention,' but Georgia quickly dismissed her wise voice because it was easier to live in denial and hope it would work out. She paused for breath, then picked up her mobile, which fortunately wasn't broken.

Why did she always go for complicated relationships when most of her friends were either engaged or married to men who were previously single? What was wrong with her? Was there a reason why she attracted emotionally unavailable men? If there was, it was time to face the truth and stop doing it!

Stewie, as she called him, according to Georgia, had been doing his best to spend time with her under difficult circumstances. There she went again, making excuses for him. Georgia's face itched. She couldn't stop scratching down the sides, not caring how red it appeared. Her friend Suzanne said it was suppressed anger. No doubt she was right because she was angry.

Georgia took some long deep breaths and started to breathe in for four, held her breath for four, then let go until she felt better. Why had she accepted this relationship into her life if it was ever that? There were worse words to describe it. A lover was one of the better ones.

The moment she met Stewie she felt magnetically drawn to him, but had it been his looks? Because he was a good-looking man. He also owned a recruitment agency, another attraction. Plus, he'd found her a job, so something had come out of this if she finally gave in and stopped fighting with herself.

The day they met was strongly embedded in Georgia's mind. She had been fed up with her job for months, and, more recently, her work had reached a pivotal point. She felt frustrated and trapped and wanted to move on to something new, but she wasn't sure what! Stewie had quickly revamped her CV, which made her appear impressive. So much so that she wondered why she'd got stuck working at Watkins & Sharpe for so long, but she'd never known anything different. Georgia had been brought up with a 'stick-at-it ethic,' which came from her father, who constantly reminded her that the grass wasn't greener on the other side of the fence. Now at twenty-eight years old, she was desperate for change. She'd worked at this firm since she left school, first as a receptionist then later as an administrator. It was boring, but she knew they valued her. Unsurprisingly, Georgia began to look for a new challenge, and the obvious thing to do was to seek the help of a recruitment agency.

The immaculately dressed Stewie cleared his throat.

'I've been going through your CV and noticed that you've been working for the same firm since you left school. Can you provide a few more details of your duties at Watkins & Sharpe? How would you describe your daily routine?' he asked, leaning forward in his chair, which had started to creak loudly.

Georgia took a long deep breath. Her head was saying boring, and she'd been distracted by the sound of the chair, which in a strange way had broken the awkwardness. Her mind flicked through her years of mundane work, and she realised that she'd have to find some inventive words to impress this man. Being put on the spot made Georgia uncomfortable. It was hard enough to focus without the distraction of the chair, Stewie's penetrating blue eyes and engaging smile.

'Well, many things, but I've done a lot more facilitating recently,' she replied, smiling back.

'Ah, facilitating, that's good,' repeated Stewie. 'Have you any HR experience? Because I've a great opportunity which is available at the end of the month, but they do require someone with experience.'

'HR, yes, I've done a little of that,' she replied, trying to avoid direct eye contact because she knew she was winging it. But what did she have to lose when the alternative was to stay stuck in her job? What a nightmare. Selling herself had never been her strong point, but she needed to push herself now. How do you do this, she thought, then remembered her yoga breathing, which had always calmed her during challenging times.

'OK, let's add that to your C.V.,' replied Stewie, giving her a further taste of his captivating smile.

'I did that cover about two years ago, so I may need some updating,' Georgia mumbled, as she took another deep breath.

'You would have training in this role because it's working for a large company, and their HR department is massive.'

'Good,' replied Georgia, who had started gazing out of the window. Why was she always so tense when she wanted to appear confident? Avoiding Stewie's gaze for a while might lighten the situation. Stewie, who was still busy taking notes, also appeared tense. She noticed it had started to rain outside and hadn't brought an umbrella. This man's flipping gorgeous, why don't I meet men like him, she thought, then noticed an expensive looking wedding ring on his finger.

Married, damn. I better not get drawn in, her wise voice reminded her, but she found it hard to dismiss her attraction when she could already feel a connection.

Stewie quickly finished making notes on his laptop, then looked up and said, 'I'll forward your C.V. to the company, and if the client gets in touch, I'll contact you.'

'Thank you,' she replied.

Two days later she had an interview with the company and, to her surprise, lunch with Stewie to discuss the position in more detail. Now, after five months of seeing each other, he was backing off or placing her on his back burner. Was that something he usually did? She'd heard my wife doesn't love me scenario, where they would stayed together to pay the mortgage, so many times it sounded like a cliché. Was she that stupid? Why couldn't she face the truth that this connection had become boring, and Stewie was hanging by a thread? Hadn't she found it hard to leave the estate agents? But as soon as she had, she felt like a different person. Diamond Class Insurance were more than happy to train her in HR. She loved her new job. Her work life rocked. Making that change had been extremely challenging, but as soon as she'd done it, her life was so much better. Until she immediately put herself into another difficult situation.

Stewie's visits had become irregular, and worse still, he was always in a hurry. He'd seldom arrive before nine p.m., and then he didn't want to stay the night. Was this what she wanted? How could it be? Had she just slid into this because he was the only male who'd taken an interest in her for a long time? But he certainly wasn't the only man, and the awakened part of Georgia knew that she deserved better.

STEWIE AND DEBS

Stewie arrived home from work. The house was untidy, and Debs was moaning about the children. Stewie was tired. He frequently arrived home after seven because he was so busy at work. He knew it was a negative habit, but he felt stuck, so there was little choice. He was constantly chasing companies to see if they needed staff, which was endless and tiring. He had some regular clients, but since Covid, not an awful lot of recruitment was taking place. Existing staff tended to stick with their current jobs because companies were allowing employees to work from home, which was fine, but it had impacted the recruitment industry.

The girls went to bed in half an hour, so he would then have a little time to himself. He wished Deborah would cheer up because she made the atmosphere heavy. Being at home was often as stressful as work. He'd quickly read a story to the girls, but then he had to eat. Hopefully, Debs had cooked something. She was often too tired to bother. If they had no dinner, they could order pizza, knock up some pasta, then go to bed, which had become their Monday-to-Friday routine.

Stewie discovered that the children were very lively, and after reading their favourite stories, they didn't want to calm down. His phone buzzed, and he noticed a text had come in from Georgia, which simply said, 'pencil me in then,' with a downward smile emoji. He decided not to respond because he'd explained how it was from the start that he'd fit her in when he could. He wanted to leave Debs, but the children were too young. There was nothing left between them apart from a little necessary conversation. She was either chatting, texting her friends, or watching Netflix, none of which interested him.

Stewie was a reader. His parents had wanted him to be a doctor, but his qualifications weren't good enough. That was him, not good enough. He wore that label. He knew he'd done well running the recruitment agency, where he had the respect and admiration of his colleagues, but he always came back to that same old feeling. They were meant to be visiting his parents on Sunday, which made things worse. His father held such high expectations of him throughout his school and university life of becoming a doctor that recruitment had never been on his radar. As far as John was concerned, he'd wasted his life getting an average degree because he didn't apply himself properly. He frequently told him that he lacked determination and could have done so much better. Stewie knew that he didn't want to work fifty hours a week as a trainee doctor, potentially more, but the irony of it was that he was now doing this in his own business and still hitting brick walls. He didn't want to hear 'I told you so,' so he tried not to discuss his work with his parents. He was happy to talk about the children because they were always interested in them. Recently, he felt that his father's aspirations had turned from him to the girls. He clearly thought that one of his daughters would be interested in the medical profession in future years. Stewie laughed. They were far too young to think about that, but he knew his own indoctrination had started early. He remembered receiving his first doctor's kit at the age of five, when he so desperately wanted roller skates. It was a devastating moment. Being an only child, he had no one to use his stethoscope on, and his few friends that played with him on Saturdays thought it was a dull present and didn't understand.

Stewie threw away the empty pizza box. At least it had arrived quickly. He'd talk to Debs and see if she still wanted to visit his parents tomorrow. If not, they could make an excuse not to go, say the girls had colds or something, and suggest another weekend.

'We've got to go,' replied Debs.

'We haven't got to do anything,' replied an exasperated Stewie.

'But they're your parents, and we haven't seen them for ages. I don't think we can make an excuse, especially when they are so good to the girls.'

'Yes, but they're not good to me, are they?'

'Stewie, stop behaving like a victim. You can stick up for yourself. If you don't like what your father says, tell him. Your mum's great. You know I get on with her.'

'Dad thinks she's nuts,' replied Stewie.

'Why? Because she's a Reiki healer? He doesn't understand. I'm surprised they're still together—a doctor and a healer, it makes me laugh,' said Debs, then giggled.

'I'm glad you find it funny. Let's go for a couple of hours, and if they invite us for dinner, we can make an excuse and leave early.'

'I do get it, Stewie, but I think we should stay for the day,' Debs insisted.

'Why are you like this about everything? It would be nice if you could support me and just say no, but it's always people-pleasing with you and keeping up appearances. I know Mum and you get on well, but couldn't you meet for coffee or something? Then I don't have to pretend that I'm okay with the way they talk,' replied Stewie, who felt extremely irritable.

'You're just being unkind now. It's not about what I want. It's also the girls. They're their grandparents, and they get excited about going.'

'Have I got a clean shirt? One of those checked casual ones that make me look like Bob the Builder?'

'I think so, but you'll have to check. I've been so tired that I haven't done a lot of washing.'

Stewie walked into the bathroom and looked at his mobile. He decided to answer Georgia's message after all, because it was going to be a very intense weekend, and he was dreading it.

If I get a cancellation, we can meet sooner, he said, adding a smiling emoji. What did people do before the emojis, he wondered. There was never a suitable one for what he wanted to say. He wanted to see Georgia, but he didn't want the complications because things were already difficult enough with Debs. Despite this, he knew she was good for him. Before he met her, he'd been a loser who hid behind his work, but at least she allowed him to be himself, and they had great fun together, which was something he seldom had with Debs.

SUNDAY AT THE PARENTS

John usually enjoyed his Sunday roasts, but he felt tense today. He wanted to talk to Stewie about his business, but he knew that it wasn't going to be easy. Deborah had indicated that things weren't going well for him, but wading in with hobnailed boots might not be the answer when Stewie was so defensive. His son wanted to do things his way, which he understood, but if only he would listen. The boy had always been bright and could have been a doctor if he'd put his mind to it, but he'd never known what he wanted. He got some second-class degree in business administration, which was all right, but it wasn't helping him now. Deborah seemed really concerned about him, not that Debs had talked to him directly, Sapphire his wife had told him that they obviously needed help.

'Sapphire!' Why on earth did she call herself that? It was an embarrassment, so was being a reiki healer, an aromatherapist perhaps, but a reiki healer! He kept quiet about it most of the time because they were like chalk and cheese, so what was the point! His wife Sapphire, who was formerly named Susan, kept herself occupied with her treatments, and according to her, she had many happy clients. Annoyingly, it was still a better option than her spending his money when her money went on fanciful things like candles, incense, spiritual books, or clothes, which made her look ridiculous! He looked up and noticed that the children were enjoying their nut roast. He wasn't sure how or when they became vegetarian but that was no doubt Sapphire's idea because she'd been vegetarian for several years now. She'd frequently offered to explain the reasons why, but he didn't want to know when eating meat was completely natural to him. It wasn't as if it was beef or lamb, it was free-range chicken; surely that wasn't so bad even if it was double the price!

'How are you getting on with things now, Stewie?' John finally managed to say as casually as he could muster.

'Not too bad,' replied Stewie, who was unwilling to go into much detail, 'but if covid hadn't happened I would have been doing a lot better by now.'

'If it wasn't for covid, I wouldn't have so many reiki clients,' whispered Sapphire, 'it's that damn jab.'

'Once again, you don't know what you're talking about. You've obviously been listening to your witchy friends. You know full well we were told to follow the science!' replied John angrily.

Debs started to feel uncomfortable, but the girls were eagerly awaiting their desserts and appeared oblivious. It had quickly become plain to her that

John didn't approve of Sapphire's reiki treatments, nor her views on covid, which had created a tense situation.

'Look, if you're in trouble financially Stewie, please let me know because I can help, but you need to consider a career change because I can't throw good money after bad.'

'What career? Dad, please, I can't go there again. I was never cut out to be a doctor, and you know it. I haven't got the patience, and I couldn't cope with the studying. Besides, I have the girls to look after now, so it's way too late for all that.'

His father didn't reply and quickly looked down at his plate to continue eating his roast. He didn't want it to go cold. Stewie could be right; it was too late. The girls appeared bright though, so one of them may be interested in the future.

'More gravy anyone?' asked Sapphire, who desperately wanted to change the subject. 'It's vegetarian, I didn't want to make two separate gravies.'

'Oh,' replied John, 'so I've had vegetarian gravy with mine, I didn't realise.'

'Exactly,' replied Sapphire, who now couldn't wait for this lunch to be over. She planned on taking the girls for a walk in the woods before they went into the pool.

'I'm going to read the paper in the conservatory unless anyone needs me,' declared John as he stood up from the table.

'We're all fine,' replied Debs, who just wanted to lie on a sun lounger by the pool. She was grateful for Sapphire's offer to take the children for a walk.

The sun was full, and Stewie and Debs at last had a little time to themselves to relax.

'I don't know how she puts up with him, he's such a control freak,' whispered Stewie, who thought his father might still be lingering despite his declaration about the newspaper.

'Sapphire does her own thing, which appears to work well for them. I'd love to try reiki. I've heard it's good for stress, and I'm stressed most of the time.'

'Yeah, I noticed. I'd like to ask John to loan me some money, but it would feel conditional, like I owe him something,' said Stewie, changing the subject.

'You would though, wouldn't you?'

'I'm not talking about the money. I would feel like I'd have to run things the way he wants.'

'Your dad's hard work. I don't know what to say to him; he makes me feel awkward.'

'Put up and shut up's his motto,' replied Stewie.

'Your mother lent me a book,' said Debs in an effort to change the subject.

'Oh, did she, one of her woo-woo books?'

'It's not woo-woo, it makes a lot of sense, and you sound like your dad.'

'It's called 'You Can Heal Your Life' by Louise Hay; it's a bestseller.'

'I've heard of that book.'

'Really, you can read it after me if you like. It helps with low self-esteem, all sorts of things.'

'I don't like reading self-help books. I enjoy crime, but Mum's obsessed with them.'

'I'm always surprised how Sapphire never moans; she just gets on with things,' replied Debs.

'She's probably found a secret lover to distract her.'

'Don't be stupid Stewie, Sapphire is fifty-five, and besides she wouldn't do that!'

* * * * *

Sapphire was worn out. It was hard work when the family visited because the girls, being only five and three, were very lively, but she enjoyed the children coming. They loved the pool and looked extremely cute with their swimming aids. Stewie was a brilliant dad, and he always came into the pool to keep an eye on them, but they loved their Nanna playing with them too. It was an extremely busy day, and the family finally left about five, and Sapphire went to tidy up the kitchen. Despite them having a dishwasher, there were still loads of things to do and items to put away. John had disappeared into the conservatory again to watch tennis. He often did this, especially after visitors. He always sat down for Sunday lunch with them but that was about it. He certainly wasn't interested in going for a walk or joining them in the pool, although he enjoyed swimming first thing in the morning before work.

Conversation had dried up between them lately, which was a great shame as they used to have such fun together. She thought about asking him to help with the clearing up, but she'd tried that many times before, and he'd produced an excuse, like he was watching a tennis match. Sapphire let out a huge sigh, then continued to put things away in the kitchen. She'd leave the BBQ for John to clean later; she had her limits!

SAPPHIRE AND GOLDILOCKS

It was Monday, and at last Sapphire had some time to herself. John had gone off for the day to play golf. He never worked on Mondays, so she decided to sort out her therapy room. She had new books, incense, and crystals. Her usual clients were booked in for tomorrow, and she needed to wash her couch covers, amongst other things, so everything was clean and fresh. Sapphire's journey into Reiki was purely coincidental, although she tried not to use that word now. She now referred to it as part of the divine plan, or 'the universe had steered her in the right direction,' when two years ago she bumped into an old friend whilst going for a routine health check. Marion had given up her part-time job in a pharmacy to work as a full-time therapist. She was a reflexologist and Reiki therapist, the two R's, she called them. Sapphire noticed that Marion's energy was great, quite different to her own. She felt that something had been missing from her life for quite some time. She hadn't worked for several years after being made redundant shortly before Covid, which had at first been a disappointment, then a relief. Her work as a manager for a large bank had been stressful, so, when they closed the branch, she gratefully took the redundancy money and bought a large cabin, which was placed at the end of the garden. The cabin was robust, with several windows. At first, she joked it was a Goldilocks cabin, as it looked like something from a fairy tale. It certainly held a special kind of magic, because after she'd added all her crystals and wands, it really came to life. John had never been in the cabin, although he joked that was where she did her voodoo. When it was first built, he was curious, so he stuck his head inside to say he wanted the largest bowl of porridge, but he'd never seen it kitted out as it was now, with therapy couch, CD player, bookshelves for her spiritual books, hanging mobiles which created beautiful light, and a big pile of incense sticks.

'Is this a new type of perfume?' he'd joke after her sessions. 'You smell like a church. I don't want to be reminded of that smell; can you take a shower?' he'd say.

'If you want me to make lunch, you'll have to put up with it,' she'd reply, and he'd normally say something like, 'OK, Goldilocks,' then laugh.

John had a good sense of humour, but in truth, he felt slightly embarrassed by his wife's radical shift in values. Any spare time they had together, without the family, Sapphire's head was stuck in a book. He preferred not to ask what the book was about; in case he got DIY psychology. If she wanted to do this, then why didn't she train as a psychologist or something? Then she could get a job at his surgery. The bright

JENNIFER LYNCH

red hair wouldn't fit too well, but at least it wasn't
blue!

Sapphire loved John, but he also bored her. She
knew he was no longer on her page, whatever her
page was. One thing was for certain: they were
moving in different directions. If it wasn't for his
sense of humour, she would have left him years ago,
but occasionally there were glimmers of the old John
shining through, which gave her hope. She'd tried on
many occasions to share her views on Covid, but
whenever she said the word, he immediately shut
her down. Fortunately, she had a few friends who
thought like her, which was a blessing. She'd formed
a spiritual development group, and they met every
Wednesday evening to meditate and chant in the
cabin. John would normally go out to play
badminton, then have a couple of drinks to keep well
out of the way. He didn't want to be anywhere near
that coven! Goldilocks had lost the plot when she
started meeting up with other weird women, some
of whom hadn't been near a GP's surgery in thirty
years!

Several weeks ago, Sapphire received a phone call
from Simon, a divorcee who was also a therapist to
one of her friends, asking if he could join her
spiritual group. Sapphire felt unsure, because the
energy of the group was expanding, and unless he
was aware, he could imbalance the whole group.
Simon explained he was a hypnotherapist who had
his own clients, so after a lengthy discussion, she
decided that he'd be a good fit, and he joined them.

As soon as Sapphire met Simon, she felt an instant recognition. It wasn't due to his physical appearance, but as they began to share conversations, she realised that he was aligned with many of her views. It was indescribable, and it left her baffled. It was also liberating not to have to wade through layers of explanations, because he just got it, plus they had read many of the same books.

Sapphire didn't want to make comparisons between him and John because her husband had stood by her for years and allowed her to do the things she wanted. He hadn't taken any of her redundancy, and he was happy for her to place the cabin wherever she chose, even though it took up a large part of the garden. But recently the 'coven jokes' had started to get out of hand. She wanted him to take her seriously. He'd never have behaved like this towards her when she worked at the bank. Was it too much to share her thoughts about Reiki and meditation with their old friends? But because John thought her work was weird and her meditation friends were quacks, he made it difficult. He'd humiliate her at the dinner table by saying, 'Goldilocks and her crazy coven. I don't know what she gets up to in there.' Sapphire wanted him to stop, but the more she asked him to let it go, the less he cared. Then there was the whole situation with their son. John didn't understand Stewie's need to set up a recruitment agency, but she knew why because it suited his personality, and he had the right qualifications for it. John was stuck in the past, and that's where he enjoyed being. Nothing was going to shift! She offered to give him Reiki when he had a painful leg last year, which went on for weeks, but she very soon realised that he'd rather limp or take painkillers than try something different.

Simon was single. He'd thought about marrying once, but he was too much of a free spirit and used to being on his own. He'd told the group that's how he liked it. He didn't plan on marrying in the future, but if he met someone, he'd want an open relationship. The Universe, according to Simon, had its own divine timing, which couldn't be hurried. If two people were on a similar path and vibration, they were likely to meet at some point. Synchronicity was where it was at, and coincidences didn't exist—that was old hat! The sooner you give up trying to make things happen by surrendering to what is, the easier life becomes. Simon appeared to go with the flow, which Sapphire found refreshing, while John couldn't cope without super-intensive planning.

John frequently talked about them going on holiday to the Maldives next year, but Sapphire wasn't sure if she wanted to go anywhere with him. It was a holiday in her cabin, a place where she could escape the mundane and think about Simon. She was married, so she vowed not to go there because of the complication. Surely, she should be happy when she had a beautiful house, a lovely son and daughter-in-law who was interested in her work, gorgeous grandchildren, a pool, a cabin, and she could do anything she wanted. But despite this, she felt ridiculed. John had been a doctor since he was twenty-five years old, and in his mid-fifties, he was confident that the NHS was the best and only way forward for ill health, apart from a few respectable therapies that were available through the surgery. However, these therapies weren't something that he'd want to try himself. John was happy with his belief system, and he didn't want to make any changes to please Sapphire.

Sapphire wondered if something odd was going on with Stewie because he'd shown so little interest in Debs at the weekend, it was as if the poor girl didn't exist. She'd hate to feel that invisible, especially when his phone was constantly buzzing. Someone was texting him a lot, at the weekend too. She hoped they weren't going to have problems because it would be bad for the grandchildren. Did Stewie have someone else, or was she imagining it? After all, she was frequently told she had a vivid imagination!

TRYING TO CHEER UP

It was now mid-October, and the weather had started to change to typical autumn weather. Debs had already put the heating on because she thought being warmer would lift her low mood. She felt ignored, frustrated, and undervalued, so her self-esteem was at an all-time low. Why couldn't Stewie recognise how tiring it was working as a part-time teacher and being the mother of two lively girls? Florence went to day care nursery, which cost them a packet because it was private, and Elsbeth was now at the primary school where she worked as a teacher, which made things a little easier, but life was still hectic, especially as the day care nursery was on the opposite side of town to the school! At three thirty she had to pack up her stuff, quickly grab Elsbeth, then head off on a twenty-minute journey to the nursery, which often took thirty minutes at that time of day. If they got away fast and didn't talk to anyone, they could arrive by three fifty, which left just enough time to collect Florence before the nursery shut at four.

Debs thought her life was like living on a conveyor belt. Fortunately, her weekends were better because Stewie was around, although he'd recently joined a local football team, which meant he trained most Saturdays. Debs found it annoying that all the girls' activities were now left to her, but despite her annoyance, she felt it was good for him to take part when he was under so much stress trying to keep on top of his business.

John had offered to buy Stewie a golf membership at his local club, but he'd declined because he thought his father would use it as an opportunity to talk about the past. He'd told Debs that the less time he spent with him, the better. It was hard visiting his parents once a month. Fortunately, the girls had become a form of defence, which deflected some of the negativity. Stewie hoped John didn't start career-guiding them instead, now or in the future, because they were far too young, but at the back of his mind he remembered the doctor's kit he'd received at Elsbeth's age, which broke his heart. He often told Debs the story that all he wanted to do was to play on roller skates in the street with the other children. Surely his parents understood that he wanted to be part of the gang, instead of having a posh present which nobody understood!

Debs continued to feel down and started avoiding mirrors. Her hair, which was now a long mousy brown, needed a colour to brighten it up. She wanted blonde streaks, anything to make it appear more interesting. Her face was pale, and she felt washed out. She'd started to pile on too many pounds (or kilos, as her scales said) by munching her way through packets of bourbon biscuits. These were meant for the girls, but several weeks ago, in her desperation for sugar, she decided she had a real liking for them because they reminded her of her childhood. Those were happy times when she and Ben watched cartoons on Saturday mornings, and her parents took care of anything that needed doing, which was total bliss! Her parenting had been good, but sadly her mother and father were both killed in a car accident before Elsbeth was born, so they never met their grandchildren. A tear ran down Debs' face. It made her extremely sad when she thought about them because the girls would no doubt have loved them. At least she had her brother Ben, but not a day went by when she didn't think about them.

The clock now said four, and Debs managed to stop herself from dunking the last two biscuits in her tea. She needed to leave some for the girls or there would be arguments. Elsbeth was playing with a school friend today, and Florence had fallen asleep on the sofa watching some brightly coloured cartoon she loved, which Debs felt would be bad for her eyes. She quickly shut the kitchen cupboard and looked at her to-do list, which had grown! Ironing—well, that could wait until tomorrow. Stewie would be back in about an hour, and no doubt he'd be starving, so she had to think about dinner. Florence also needed to wake up or she'd never sleep tonight. They could go for a quick trip to the park, which was only a ten-minute walk, then she'd start making a quiche.

As she walked past the hallway mirror, she caught a look at herself and was shocked. What had happened to her? She had lost sight of herself! She used to be so happy and full of life, glowing, people said, particularly when she was pregnant—and she now resembled a woman much later in life! No wonder Stewie wasn't interested in her. Debs felt desperate to do something about her appearance, but she wasn't sure what would help. Did she need therapy? Sapphire's reiki sounded good; she could give it a try. Or there was this magic man that her friend couldn't stop talking about. According to Denise, Simon was a brilliant hypnotherapist who not only helped you to remove feelings of negativity but also connected to past lives. Debs thought the past life work sounded unsettling, a little weird and unconventional. Sapphire believed in that sort of thing, but she wasn't sure if she did. If she had therapy with Simon, then she certainly wouldn't say anything to Stewie. If he thought his mum's books were woo-woo, what on earth would he make of past lives!

GEORGIA – FINDS HER VOICE

It was the seventeenth of October, and Georgia received a text from Stewie to say he'd be over at eight thirty this evening, which she knew would be closer to nine. Georgia lived in a shared house on the west side of town where the properties were more affordable, and Stewie lived on the east side, which was considered upmarket. The wait had been difficult this time, but at least he'd texted to confirm he was coming. They were ordering a Chinese, which Stewie was picking up on the way over. After all her waiting, Georgia wasn't sure if she wanted to see him tonight, but they still needed to talk. She'd rehearsed what she was going to say: their relationship wasn't going anywhere, and with him being married, it was no longer right for her. Plus, if her parents found out that she was seeing a married man, they would go mental. Georgia knew her reputation was at risk, which made her uncomfortable and constantly on edge, and it no longer seemed fair to be under that pressure.

Stewie arrived in a new shirt with a light jacket, and Georgia instantly thought how attractive he looked! He explained that he'd come straight over from work and had told Debs he was going out with some of the guys from football, so it wasn't a problem for them to spend a few hours together.

'I missed you,' he said as he slid his arms around her and kissed her on the cheek. 'Thank God for my Georgia.'

Georgia felt triggered because, sadly, she knew she wasn't his anything, not his girlfriend or wife. She was his bit on the side, and she felt like a caged animal that Stewie now put on a pedestal, as if she held some special place. He put on his playlist. He always did this, not bothering to ask what she might want to listen to. He assumed that she wanted the same as him, or he didn't care. To be fair, Stewie loved soul music, particularly seventies soul, which she didn't mind, so she decided not to mention it. Why bother when he was in his element, and she wanted him to be happy?

The Chinese was still hot, and Stewie spread it out on the coffee table to eat out of the containers. Georgia inwardly cringed. Somehow, it spoiled the taste to eat it out of plastic boxes, but Stewie explained that's what they always did when they had Chinese at home. They often had takeaways because Debs hardly cooked, being exhausted most of the time. Georgia tucked into her vegetable chow mein. The Chinese was good, and the spring rolls were perfect. She called herself vegetarian, but she still ate a little seafood, and on the odd occasion fish.

Stewie felt tired. Debs appeared annoyed when he told her he was going out tonight, but it wasn't his fault she didn't have a life! She had opportunities to go out if she wanted. She had friends, people she worked with, women from her yoga class, although he hadn't seen her go there for ages and she'd put on a load of weight. She appeared depressed. He wanted to talk about it to Georgia, who was a great listener (a natural empath), but he liked keeping the two sides of his life in different boxes. Otherwise, it became confusing. Besides, Georgia was looking hot in an unconventional way tonight, so why waste time discussing Debs?

Georgia wore a short dress with thick leggings and a loose cardigan over the top. It was a cold house, and no doubt the radiators needed bleeding or something. Rented rooms they were all the same, although this room was spacious, and Georgia had a double bed. They also had use of the kitchen. If they saw her roommates, she told them Stewie was a friend from work, although the comments they made confirmed that they didn't believe a word of it!

'It's a great Chinese,' said Georgia at last. She'd been going over what she was going to say to Stewie dozens of times, and now she had the opportunity to speak, and all she did was comment on the food. Could she do this when she was so weak and undisciplined? Stewie had helped her to find a job, which changed her life, but she didn't owe him anything, so why was it this hard? Before she had the chance to speak, Stewie jumped in.

'My marriage is over. I'm going to leave in January. It would be terrible to go before then, when the girls are so excited about Christmas—especially Elsbeth. It has begun even earlier since she started school. We are still in October; would you believe it?'

Suddenly, Georgia's plan to let Stewie know she was leaving had been turned on its head. He obviously was serious about her because he was finally going to take that step and leave Debs. But what did this mean for her? No doubt she'd have to wait another three months to see if he really did it. Then where would he live? Stewie had always said that they didn't have any money, as it all went on the mortgage, bills, and the girls.

'Really, Stewie, have you taken the time to think this through? Can you afford to leave right now, and where would you live? You realise that this will have a devastating effect on Debs and the girls, plus your parents will be horrified!'

'I know that, Georgia. I haven't come to this decision overnight. You know I want to be with you. I don't want Debs or the girls to be hurt, but there's nothing between us anymore. It's like being married to an alien. Something has got to change because we can't carry on as we are. We're killing each other—physically and emotionally.'

'I get that, Stewie, but where are you going to live? You can't afford to rent a house. Rents are horrendous in Bristol unless you happen to earn loads of money.'

'I thought I'd move in here until I find something. It wouldn't be permanent, just until we can get a place together.'

Georgia's heart was beating uncontrollably fast. Stewie was triggering her left, right, and centre, and she felt stressed. This wasn't how she envisaged their relationship going. For some reason, she'd always thought that Stewie would look after her not the other way around and now he'd asked to share her tiny space! There were four people in this house already, including herself, and the landlord had made it clear to them on many occasions that there mustn't be five. No one's boyfriend or girlfriend was allowed to move in because it pushed up the bills, which he included in their rent. This had to be no because it would destabilise her living arrangements.

'What do you think, my Georgia? I could move in over the New Year. You have that time off work then, don't you? So, you could help me. I can't wait to get out of there. You're not that far away, so I could pop back and see the kids. It would be a brand-new start for us.' Stewie looked at Georgia and wondered why she wasn't saying anything. This wasn't like her. Surely, she wanted them to be together. He went to put his arms around her and hold her close to get a reaction.

'It won't work, Stewie.'

'What do you mean by that? You love me, don't you? You're always telling me that. I thought you wanted us to be together.'

'Not like this,' Georgia replied, with tears rolling down her face, 'not at the expense of Debs and your girls.'

'How did you think it was going to happen?'

'I've no bloody idea—but not like this. I was stupid enough to think that you'd find your own place first. Then we'd be together when you were settled, but to move straight in with me is madness. Can't you see there isn't enough room here? I do everything in this small room, and you think I could cope with you here as well?'

'Alright, I get it. But there's no need to get stroppy. If you won't help me, then I'll have to think of another way.'

Georgia stood up and started to put the greasy Chinese containers in a black bin liner to take to the dustbin.

'Just go, Stewie. I was going to tell you we were over before all this happened. I want to be on my own. You're a lovely person, but I don't need all this baggage.'

'Baggage? You're the one with baggage, Georgia. You were the girl who came to my recruitment agency looking for a job. You wouldn't say boo to a goose. You'd only ever worked for one employer, and you were afraid to leave because you were worried about what people thought of you. I thought your motto was 'stick at it,' but you don't want to stick with me? I gave you the confidence you needed, and now you've shot me in the foot!'

'Don't be such a drama queen, Stewie. You're the one with low self-esteem—you're always saying how you feel second best to your father—but you'll never stand up to him, nor Debs. You just moan about them. It's never your fault when things don't work out. I'm sorry, Stewie. I've had enough. I don't want this.'

Stewie was angry. Georgia talked to him like some sad victim who had no control over his life. Well, he did and if she wanted him to leave, he would. They were done for good this time. They would had a few arguments before, but nothing like this. How dare she comment on his family like that when she didn't know anything about them?

'Goodbye, Georgia. It was great while it lasted,' he said, grabbing his coat that he'd slung over the end of the sofa.

Georgia felt upset and wanted to shout, 'I'm sorry, please don't go. I didn't mean it,' but she did and the wise woman part of her that had been buried for so long had finally surfaced. She heard Stewie slam the front door and try to start his Audi, which took several attempts before it was running. 'Fuck you then,' she shouted, swearing until she felt better. Surprisingly, she no longer felt tearful. All she felt was relief, because out of nowhere a huge surge of energy came in, which she could only describe as energetic realisation. If this was empowerment, it was amazing!

STRUGGLING WITH ROUTINE

Debs had a busy day at school. It wasn't long until half term, but her class was already restless and tired. Teaching seven-year-olds had its challenges, but deep down she loved it. There were just these difficult days and today appeared to be one of them. She also had a headache, which started when she left home and had persisted most of the morning, plus she was teaching recorder group in half an hour. She took some painkillers with a glass of water. The children were currently learning maths, which wasn't her favourite subject to teach because some of them really struggled and needed extra help, but there were never enough teaching assistants to go around. Fortunately, by the time she'd organised the recorder group, her headache had begun to subside. It was only an hour until lunch break, when she would have the opportunity for fresh air.

The staffroom was completely empty, and Debs helped herself to a coffee from the machine, which had been purchased in recent weeks. It was slower than the kettle, but the coffee was delicious, and she took a sip of latte, which was hot! Her phone buzzed and there was a message from Simon, which said, 'I can fit you in tomorrow at seven. Let me know if you can make it, and I'll leave you the directions to my flat where I work in the evenings. Best wishes, Simon.'

Simon's quick response surprised Debs. She felt as if she'd put her toe in the water and didn't know how deep it went. Would she be safe on her own with this man? She should be because he was a professional. Sapphire had mentioned what a great guy he was when she'd talked about him in her group. Initially, she hadn't linked them, but when she contacted him, she realised there couldn't be that many Simons who were hypnotherapists in Bristol. She was being silly because her friend was already having treatments with him and was happy. Anyway, she'd decided to go, so she quickly replied to his message to say that time was fine, and she'd think about what to say Stewie. She might just tell him the truth and take the ridicule. He'd be okay; he was just a little out of his comfort zone with her doing things he didn't understand. Debs finished her coffee. If she was honest with herself, she had needed help for a long time and now, at least, she was doing something about it. Simon told her that it would take five or six sessions to notice the results, and that she could come once a fortnight. It was expensive, but then again, she had some savings. It was difficult for her to spend four hundred pounds or so on herself when there were so many things that the girls needed, but there seemed to be no other way forward because if one of them didn't act soon, they would end up splitting up. Debs knew that she and Stewie still loved each other, but their relationship was fast dissolving under the pressure they faced with Stewie's business. He'd put in so many hours and was coming home late, yet despite all his hard work, their family budget was shrinking. He had business loans up to his ears to keep things going. Was it all worth it? But if he didn't continue with the agency, what would he do? It would be difficult for them to manage on her salary alone. She might have to work full time, and she was tired enough as it was.

The bell went to signify the end of lunch break, and Debs returned to class. The time had gone by so quickly that she hadn't been outside. She'd been reading up on her lesson plans, which was challenging when her head was so full. It felt like loads of voices were jabbering at the same time, and she'd lost her ability to think straight. Where was her navigation? She certainly wasn't the clear-thinking person she was before meeting Stewie, but that was years ago now. Debs had always considered herself an intelligent and fun-loving person who loved her teaching work, but now she was dragging herself around. She wondered if Stewie was with someone else when he didn't come home until after ten last night. Had she smelt perfume on him when he came to bed? She hadn't been close enough to him to be certain! There had been restless energy about him, and he seemed annoyed. She'd asked him what was up, but he just mumbled he was okay, and he'd just had a bad day. Everyone had bad days, didn't they? Was she letting her thoughts get out of hand? But as she left the staff room her headache resurfaced, and Debs was having a meltdown. Thank God she'd booked Simon. I hope he can help, she whispered as the children dragged their chairs across the floor.

The next day, Debs decided to tell Stewie the truth because she didn't like lying, and white lying wasn't acceptable either. She'd never been that type of person, and he'd find out eventually, so she went for it!

'Why? It isn't as if you smoke or anything! Weight loss, I could understand. I know you're depressed, but surely you would be better seeing the doctor, he could put you on anti-depressants or something. Do we have the money for this sort of thing? I thought we were saving for a week away early next year,' replied Stewie.

Debs knew Stewie's reaction wouldn't be good and she had to fight against her people-pleasing pattern and acknowledge that she needed something for herself, which she found exceedingly difficult. If she thought too long and hard about it, she wouldn't go. It was true they were meant to be saving for a holiday, but so far, they only had a hundred pounds in the kitty, which she'd put in the pot because Stewie didn't have any money. Besides, she was using her own money to pay for the hypnotherapy. She needed to use some of her Tauren stubbornness. If she didn't change, she was going to stay stuck, and that clearly wasn't healthy.

'I'm going tonight at seven, so can you please look after the girls? I'll be back around nine, so I won't be late!' she replied, feeling her desperation.

Stewie looked disgruntled. He'd planned on working until eight and then popping over to see Georgia. If he turned up unexpectedly on her doorstep, he might be able to persuade her to rethink their relationship, although she had seemed adamant they were over.

'Do what you like, Debs, I need to get off to work. I don't work part time like you do!' he shouted, grabbing his coat and slamming the door behind him.

The Audi wouldn't start again. What more could go wrong, Stewie thought impatiently. It was one thing Debs and him were hardly talking, but now she was going down the same route as Sapphire! For one moment he almost felt compassion for his father, then it left. That old bugger didn't deserve it. Georgia didn't deserve him either, not after the things she'd said. To think he was planning on leaving Debs and the children to be with her, and she didn't even want him! Stewie felt the pain of rejection and was angry. He needed to get to work on time today because he had an important meeting with a company who planned on taking several new staff on. One more turn of the key, and it started. God was on his side for a change if nobody else was!

SIMON'S HYPNOTHERAPY SESSION

Simon explained to Debs the process she'd go through in detail and reassured her that if she appeared at all distressed, he'd quickly bring her back. Debs described what was going on at home, with Stewie and the girls and her marriage in general. She said that she felt lonely and ignored by Stewie most of the time, and now they were hardly communicating. He asked about her family and Debs told him how she had lost her parents while pregnant with Elsbeth, and that she hardly saw her brother because he lived in Scotland, and she didn't have enough time to visit him. She noticed that Simon was very thorough in taking notes. He explained that her soul guidance would bring up whatever was needed, and she wasn't to worry because he'd be talking to her the whole time.

Debs felt comfortable and began counting backwards from thirty. She heard fifteen, and after that, she was in such a deeply relaxed state that she lost track of numbers. It was dark, but she could see a glimmer of light in the distance as if that was the way out. She then became aware of Simon's voice.

'I want you to remember how you felt directly after the accident. Are you angry, and do you want to say anything to your parents?' he asked.

'I'm angry because I don't understand why they left me when I'm pregnant with their grandchild. I feel so alone.'

'Do you feel they abandoned you?' continued Simon.

'Yes, I feel frustrated that I haven't told them I'm pregnant.'

'What would you like to say to them?'

'I'd like to tell them how much I love them, and that I'm having their grandchild, and I'm extremely sad that they won't be here for me when I have the baby.' Debs suddenly became aware that tears were streaming down her face.

'Can you forgive them for leaving you, and would you like to talk to them?' asked Simon.

For a moment, Debs's rationality kicked in, and she doubted it was possible. Then she decided to say, 'Yes, I would,' as it felt like the obvious thing to do.

'I'm going to bring in your parents. They might have something to say to you too, so be open to that and stay in love.' A few minutes later Simon said, 'They are with us now.'

'I can feel them, and I can see them as they used to be. They are wearing the same clothes,' said Debs, who now felt very relaxed.

'Yes, they are here with us, and they are fine on the other side. I will leave you to talk to them for a few minutes, and then I'll come in and help you say goodbye,' explained Simon reassuringly.

Debs held her parents tightly, and they quickly responded by putting their arms around her. 'I'm sorry that I've been angry, but I felt abandoned. I was pregnant with Elsbeth when you left, and I felt so alone.'

'Deborah, you've never been alone. We're here with you, and we see you every day. We see Elsbeth and Florence, they are such beautiful girls. We know you are lonely and not getting on well with Stewart, but things will improve. He has much to learn and despite what you feel right now, he is learning, and things will change in the future for you both,' said her mother. Her communication was loud and clear, and it felt telepathic. Then her father said, 'Your mother's right. I know how difficult it was for you, but we're here even if you can't see us. We are always with you You are strong and beautiful and there are many great things to come, you will see and soon. Don't worry about Stewart. He chose a difficult path, but we're helping him also. Love and blessings to you both.'

Debs became aware of Simon's voice coming in, which startled her. She was so comfortable in this place that she didn't want to return, but she had to return for the girls.

'Deborah, say goodbye to your mum and dad, and listen to my voice because it's time to come back now,' Simon said reassuringly.

They slowly began to separate. While Debs was waving goodbye to her parents, she became aware that her vision of them was becoming smaller and more distant. She then heard Simon counting, twenty-five, twenty-four, and the counting continued while Debs slowly opened her eyes. After a few minutes of being quite motionless, Debs slowly moved herself to a sitting position and Simon passed her a glass of water and smiled. She was speechless and very thirsty. After putting down the glass on the little table next to the couch she went to step down to the floor.

'No, don't get up yet, stay where you are, and relax for ten minutes. You've been on quite a journey, and you need to come down to earth slowly, so take your time.'

Debs glanced at her watch. It was half past eight. Where did the time go? She couldn't believe she'd been in this session for forty minutes. Her mobile had been silent, so she turned it on, and immediately noticed a text from Stewie, but decided not to read it and returned her phone to her handbag.

'How are you feeling?' asked Simon.

'Wow, I feel incredible. It felt as if my parents were standing in the room with me. I feel relieved, imagine them knowing about the girls. I never believed in this sort of thing, but what they said reassured me that they're around me all the time. I felt a huge amount of love coming from them. I've had many conversations with Sapphire about similar things, but I thought she was deluded.'

'Sapphire? Is she your mother-in-law? The lady you mentioned earlier, who's a reiki healer and runs a spiritual development group?' asked Simon.

'Yes, I think you're in her group, she's mentioned you.'

'Oh, that Sapphire! Yes, it's a great group, you ought to come.'

'Perhaps when we've finished our sessions,' she replied.

'You might find that you feel a little tired over the next few days, while the energies integrate, but I'm sure you'll notice some big changes.'

'Things need to change,' whispered Debs. 'Anyway, I think I ought to make a move now. It was difficult enough for me to come, but I'll make another appointment for a fortnight.'

'Great. see you then,' replied Simon as he accompanied her to his front door.

What an amazing man, and beautiful flat, thought Debs. The pictures of angel wings on his walls, and the crystals and candles had fascinated her, plus he had a huge dreamcatcher hanging over the therapy couch in beautiful colours. He'd also given her a piece of hematite for grounding, which he told her to put in her pocket or sock. She did feel different as if something had really shifted inside her and she felt supported, not so alone. It felt as if her parents were still around her and she was protected. That was strange, but then the whole experience had been odd. It had opened her up to things that she never believed were possible. She couldn't wait to tell Sapphire about it because it would make them closer. One thing was for sure, she wasn't going to say anything too much to Stewie because he wouldn't believe her, and no doubt she'd be given the same delusional label as his mother!

Debs quickly arrived home, and walked into the hallway, which was noticeably quiet. She didn't want to shout, 'I'm back,' in case it woke the girls. She walked over to the kettle to make a cup of tea. After her drink, she'd check on the girls, then go to bed, which would avoid any deep conversations about tonight. The lounge was empty, and it didn't sound like Stewie was having a shower, so she sat down on the sofa with her tea and opened the text that he'd sent earlier. 'I'm going out for a quick drink with a mate, so don't wait up. I've asked Poppy to pop over until you're back.' Debs put down her empty cup and headed for the girls' room where she found Poppy looking at the girls' storybooks. 'I love these stories; they remind me of when I was little. Sorry, I didn't hear you come in, or I would have come down,' she said cheerfully.

'Thanks for coming at short notice, Poppy. I hope Stewie paid you?'

'Yeah, he gave me twenty quid. The girls were already asleep when I came over, but I've been up to check on them a few times.'

'Ok great,' whispered Debs, who didn't want to wake her daughters up when they were sleeping so peacefully. She couldn't believe that Stewie wouldn't wait for her to return before he went out! He must have been desperate to go, or he was trying to prove a point about her not being home. She seldom went anywhere, so what was his problem! Debs took a long deep breath. Surprisingly, she found that she didn't care if Stewie was in or not, when normally she felt quite anxious about him being out having fun, when she was stuck at home with the girls. She adored her children and wanted to spend time with them, but the fact she was usually too tired to 'have a life' got to her.

Debs surprised herself by quickly putting her phone away and picking up her book. She was going to begin the woo-woo book that Sapphire had given her tomorrow, but she decided to have a little flick through it before going to bed. 'You Can Heal Your Life' had suddenly transformed from read-it-sometime-in-the-future to essential reading because she was now on the first step of her healing journey. Wow, what an incredible man Simon is, she thought, hoping that she didn't get a crush on him, because it was obvious Sapphire had!

DEBS TRANSFORMATION
(three weeks later)

The hairdressing salon bustled with life as Debs flicked through some magazines looking for a style which would suit her. It was now half term so there was no school today, and Poppy had offered to look after the girls this morning, which was a great help. Debs decided that nurturing herself was the way forward, and she wanted a new look, a style that would lift her to make her look and feel younger! After much discussion with Shona, who she hadn't seen for over a year, she decided to have her hair layered and dyed blonde with the addition of some red highlights. By the time she left the salon two hours later, there had been a shocking transformation. When she arrived home and looked in the hall mirror and added a little lipstick and mascara, the overall result was amazing, and Debs hardly recognised herself. She was aware that she still needed to focus on cutting out snacks, particularly the girls' biscuits, but at least she'd taken the first step towards outer transformation. Her inner transformation was an ongoing process, which involved her attending yet more hypnotherapy sessions with Simon. Debs had recently been for her second one. During this session, they would explored why it didn't feel right to look after herself, where this had come from, and why she abandoned herself. They also looked at past patterns from her childhood. Her brother Ben appeared continually bright while she constantly struggled. She had found it almost impossible to obtain her teaching qualifications because her low self-esteem had become a huge obstacle.

Debs had always believed Ben was their parents' favourite, although Ben never acted as if he was superior, she held on to the belief that in comparison she'd underachieved. There was an underlying pattern of 'what's the point,' and when it came to her needs she was used to putting herself last. Now Stewie and the girls' needs came before her own. Since last week's hypnotherapy session, Debs had already started to feel differently about herself. There was no longer the feeling of a gaping hole inside her when she thought about her life. It surprised her how quickly she'd booked the appointment at the hairdresser's, and she was glad she had. Her desire for biscuits had also begun to subside! When she looked at them, they now made her feel slightly sick. She'd started snacking on fruit and drinking more water. She realised that most of the work had to be done by herself. Simon offered support and help, he'd kickstarted the transformation, but she had to make the changes. Debs was already feeling so different that it gave her the courage to push on. A third session was now booked, and she eagerly awaited what they would explore next. One thing was for sure, Stewie was going to have a huge surprise when he came home from work, whatever time that might be, as recently he'd been arriving home stupidly late. Was it going to be too late to turn things around? Simon had explained that things could change, but they both had to want it. Did Stewie want to sort things out, or did he have something else going on? He'd been unrecognisable lately, not in his appearance, but his behaviour. He seemed so cold and indifferent towards her, although he was still great with the girls. It was time for change. She would do what she could, but he still had to meet her halfway, and this involved him opening up his feelings to her. It felt like the problem was more than his work; there was something else. Perhaps if they thought of a way to solve the financial issues it would be a start.

'Wow, your hair looks beautiful,' said a surprised Poppy.

'Thanks, luv. I'm going to try and keep it like this now, but it will take work.'

'No, I don't think so, it looks easy to manage. I trained to be a hairdresser, but I didn't like it, too much bitchy behaviour, so I got a job in an office, which suits me better. Although I sometimes wonder if I had continued with it, I would have enjoyed it because it's far more creative! I did pick up a few tips though, so if you ever need any help with your hair, I'd be happy to show you.'

'Gosh, you're a girl of many talents. I'll remember that, Poppy. Thank you so much for looking after the girls at short notice. I might need you again next week when I go for hypnotherapy, I'll let you know at the weekend if that's ok.' She suddenly felt light and cheerful. She'd promised the girls that if they were good while she was gone, she'd take them to the local leisure centre to play on the bouncy castles and play equipment, but they would need to have lunch before their session, which began at two.

'Mummy, you look so pretty. I want my hair like that,' said Elsbeth.

'We'll see,' Debs replied. It was the easiest thing to say, otherwise there was always a when! It was an interesting word, which she often repeated when thinking of Stewie. When will he notice me, when will he talk to me, and when will he come to bed at the same time as me. She hated that word, it made her feel awful, or did it? Something had changed inside her. It was as if the word 'when' had suddenly become less relevant because her own needs had become far more important.

JOHN AND STEWIE IN SCOTLAND

John packed up his clubs. Scotland was a long way, but the country was full of fantastic golf courses, and he had a fast car. He'd asked Stewart a few days ago if he wanted to join him on the trip because he knew he'd benefit from the break. Stewart didn't have to play golf if he wasn't interested, as there were plenty of great places to visit nearby. It was a long and boring drive on his own, but if Stewie came, they could have a father and son chat during the trip. He'd decided he was going to offer him twenty thousand and take it out of his Will. He could give ten thousand to each of the girls instead. It would help them with their university fees, medical school, whatever they did!

John was bowled over when Stewart said yes to joining him for the weekend. He was happy to be away for a few days and said he'd watch some golf, but he'd also tour around a little while the matches were on. It would be good to have a break because he hadn't had any time off in months. John had booked the hotel next to the golf club on the banks of Loch Lomond, which was his favourite. He'd visited the club about five years ago, and he had friends who played there. The views over the loch were stunning and he knew that as soon as they arrived, Stewart would feel better. It was time for a rethink about where his life was headed. He also had to work out where his relationship was going with Sapphire! Over the past few months, Sapphire had spent most of her time in that cabin and had shown little interest in going on holiday anywhere with him, let alone the Maldives, because she hadn't mentioned the holiday since he'd suggested it. Susan, as he preferred to call her, used to be keen on going away for holidays together, but Susan had been a different person! Since her change to Sapphire, many things had altered. For one, there was a young man who attended the coven who appeared to have taken her attention. Was he a wizard? The thought of this amused him, but he still felt annoyed. It was ridiculous because he was hardly a threat, just another whacko who believed in the same things she did, even past lives! Sapphire hadn't mentioned this directly, but he'd seen her head stuck in a book about it and she'd also shared some of her newfound cultism with Debs, who had started going down the same slippery slope! Initially, he'd found Sapphire's behaviour slightly amusing, but in recent months he missed the old Susan, the woman who gave him cuddles at night and wanted to hear what sort of day he had. Whereas Sapphire was totally consumed by something else and he wasn't sure how to fix it. He thought they would get back to normal over time, but the only normal he had in his life was his golf, so he'd thrown himself into it. He wanted to focus on beating his personal best. He'd become very fit with all these rounds at the golf course, even Stewie (he hated that name also) had commented on how fit and well he looked!

John packed the car. They were leaving at eight thirty, straight after breakfast. He'd have left a little earlier, but he wanted to be considerate to Stewart, who had a ton of things to do before he was ready to leave. It was now the week after half term, so the roads should be clear. He'd packed some thick jumpers, being late October, plus it was always cooler in Scotland, and he'd advised Stewie to do the same. He quickly topped up his oil, checked his tyre pressures with his gauge and after deciding everything was ok, put his case and clubs in the car with a bottle of water and flask of coffee. He could never be without his coffee on a long journey. Hopefully, if he put his foot down, they could be there by late afternoon. There weren't any matches until the following day, so they would have time to relax and eat a good dinner. The hotel was a beautiful old Georgian building, with gorgeous rooms and high ceilings that he knew Stewart would appreciate. His spirits had lifted at the thought of it, and he couldn't wait to get on the golf course.

'Hi Dad, shall I put my case in the boot?' asked Stewie, who had thankfully arrived on time.

'Yeah, just mind the clubs,' replied John. 'All ok at home? I hope Deborah didn't mind me dragging you off for a long weekend?'

'No, she didn't. Debs is a different person recently. She's more interested in those books Sapphire gave her than what I'm up to, and she's started going for hypnotherapy. It's having a positive effect on her, which makes my life easier,' replied Stewie.

'Great, let's get going, then we'll arrive in good time. We can stop somewhere for lunch along the way because I know of one or two places that do great food.'

Stewie hopped in the car and closed his door. He hadn't seen John this cheerful for a long time, but then again, he'd never been on a golfing holiday with him! John put the car radio on to Radio 2, which pleased Stewie as he often listened to that. There's some life in the old bugger yet, he thought. Stewie felt so tired that he soon drifted off to sleep, and when he awoke, he noticed they were driving past the outskirts of Birmingham.

'We'll stop for a quick coffee soon; you've been asleep for over an hour. Everything catches up with us sometimes, doesn't it?' John remarked.

'Yeah, it sure does. I think I might have a go at golf. I've been down the driving range a few times recently. I'd have to play in a beginner's match or something, we'll see, because I want to get a boat around the loch tomorrow and another day exploring the centre of Glasgow. Are these matches long?'

'Yes, some of them are, but do as you wish, I can always meet you back at the hotel for dinner. The food in their restaurant is first class. You can eat whenever you like, but I'm happy to pay for both of us to have breakfast and dinner together.'

Stewie thought about the takeaway pizzas and knock-together pasta that he and Debs ate late at night that often left him with indigestion and smiled. 'Actually, I'd love to have dinner with you Dad,' he replied as a huge feeling of relief took over him. This weekend could be great fun and a chance for them to heal some old wounds, he thought, feeling positive.

'There's something else I want to talk to you about, don't worry I'm not going to mention the doctor thing again, but I would like to help you out with your existing business. I've been thinking how badly Covid impacted you and that you've been putting so much hard work into rebuilding things, so I'd like to give you twenty thousand to kickstart your business or re-start your kickstart if that's a thing!'

Stewie was dumbfounded. 'I don't know what to say Dad, it seems like an awful lot of money. Are you sure you can do this?'

'Son, if I wasn't sure, I wouldn't offer. I'd like to help because I believe in you, and I've recently heard some great reports about your agency. I'm sorry that I didn't help you before but part of me was stuck in the past and I selfishly imagined that you are someone you're not. I get it now. Let's stop for that coffee. I'll pull over at the next garage and you can get one of those cappuccino things. I've brought my flask, but I'm not sure what's in it, hopefully proper coffee, although Lady Macbeth might have made me some poisonous brew! You may laugh son, but wait until Debs joins the coven, I'm sure it won't be long.'

Stewie smiled, then opened the door to fetch a latte. 'Back in a few minutes Dad,' he said. For once he felt almost happy, the wall between himself and John had at last started to crumble, which gave him a feeling of newfound optimism. He'd been completely bowled over by his dad's offer of help. Had he heard an apology for trying to push him into a career that he didn't want? He couldn't believe his father's change of heart. Someone or something must have influenced him, or he'd realised it was never going to happen.

Stewie returned to the car and noticed John hadn't moved. He must have a stronger bladder than me, he thought. He was busy talking to Sapphire on his mobile. Stewie wondered why he hadn't just texted, then he remembered that his father didn't like text. He said it was impersonal, and his fingers were far too big for those stupid keys.

'We're making great progress Lady Macbeth. We've just stopped for a coffee, so I thought I'd give you a call. It tastes a little weird though. You haven't poisoned me, have you?' John joked.

'No, not the coffee, but I did put a flower remedy in your bottle of water. Beech, but you shouldn't be able to taste it.'

'That's like the vegetarian gravy, I didn't notice anything different there either! Stewie's been drinking my water too, so let's hope it improves our performance!'

'Yes, it should be a good weekend, enjoy yourselves,' replied Sapphire.

Sapphire's wishes surprised John, so he suddenly said, 'Enjoy your weekend too Susan,' then turned to Stewie with 'Let's hit the road Jack,' and they sped off.

Only another five or so hours to go, thought Stewie, who had turned the car radio to Radio 4 and was surprised by how quickly they both became absorbed. It felt like a new beginning for them both and, surprisingly, he felt comfortable.

STUCK IN A BOOK

Sapphire had been reading about past lives, which she found fascinating. Her book explained that you can feel an instant connection with some people, while others, you may get on well with them, but you may not have the same familiar feeling or understand each other so easily. She found it hard to deny her attraction to Simon and thought it was likely they would have shared a past life together. Sapphire was certain he felt the same way because of the way he looked at her. He knew she was married, so it was unlikely that he'd risk his reputation by stepping over that boundary, but they were magnetically drawn together, and she found it impossible to stop thinking about him. She was still a little perplexed as to why Debs would see him for therapy when there were many therapists who could help her. She and Stewie were no doubt having problems but Debs spending time with Simon made her feel uneasy and a little exposed. She was worried that she'd say something about her that he wouldn't like! She'd always portrayed herself as a teacher within the group and she didn't want Simon to see her in a different light. Still, she had to remind herself that it was none of her business what Debs did or said, because she had the right to go for therapy, especially if it helped her. Sapphire began to question whether she had a feeling of 'I wish it was me,' lurking beneath this. If she did, then she was being childish, but she couldn't help it, when she secretly wanted to spend more time with Simon. Her feelings were moving into dangerous territory, a place she didn't want to go. She could pretend all she like that Simon was just a member of her spiritual community, but he was different to the others. They knew each other, they recognised each other's souls, and she didn't know what to do about it.

It was nearly three and Debs arrived for her reiki session. She'd decided that it would be a good opportunity to spend some time with her mother-in-law while Stewie and John were away, plus Poppy was happy to do a two-hour babysit. She needed some me time and thought it was fantastic that Stewie had agreed to go with John. If he could make some headway with his father during this trip, that would be great, at least she wouldn't have to *constantly hear him talking about the past*. He needed the hypnotherapy more than she did, but she knew that he'd never admit it. Stewie was *stuck in a rut* of his own making but hopefully this weekend would be the start of *dissolving some barriers* for him.

Sapphire greeted Debs with a long hug. The therapy bed was already set up with a beautiful cover and a gorgeous smell of incense filled the room. A few small candles were placed on a shelf next to the couch. Sapphire explained that she only used a few tealights because she couldn't risk a fire in her cabin. She produced a notepad and began to take a few notes. Despite knowing Debs well, she still had to take her medical history, details of her doctor and any medications she was on for insurance purposes. Sapphire sensed that Debs' mood was low. She asked about her lifestyle and how she felt on a scale of one to ten. Debs replied she felt around six because she was anxious about Stewie's work. He put in hours of work and still didn't appear to be moving forward. Sapphire looked up.

'If we can lift you with some reiki, I think it will help. Let's *focus on just you* during the session. Hopefully, John and Stewie will have a good weekend and between all the golf and beers, some decisions about the business can be made,' Sapphire suggested encouragingly.

'I'm happy to talk about me, I've felt better since the hypnotherapy sessions. It's really helped with the way I think about my parents, all I feel is love now and not regrets. We had unresolved business, but we managed to shift this in a few sessions, and I feel lighter and freer from the past,' replied Debs.

'But you only feel a six, are you sure it's just Stewie's work?'

'No, he has someone else. I've caught him texting someone and being very secretive. I don't have any evidence; it's just a feeling, a kind of knowing.'

'*Intuition*, I understand that! How does he feel about the hypnotherapy sessions?' asked Sapphire.

'To be honest, I don't think he likes it. When I returned from the first one, he'd gone out. I was really surprised at that. He couldn't wait for me to return before going out himself and he knew I'd be back at nine, so he'd called in Poppy from next door. I was shocked when I couldn't find him anywhere, then I found his text to say he was going for a drink with a friend, if that was true?'

'How do you feel about Simon?'

'What do you mean, how do I feel about him? He's a therapist and a professional. I found him at the time I needed help. I was going around in circles; I was an emotional mess! It was hard for me when my parents were in that crash and they never knew about their first grandchild but unbelievably, they do.

'Simon's an amazing man; he comes to our Wednesday evening group. You're welcome to join us if you're interested. How are you getting on with the book?'

'The book's amazing, I've nearly finished it. It sounds like you really like Simon.'

'I do like him; he's a fascinating young man and he has so much spiritual knowledge. When we first met, I felt as if I knew him, but it often feels like that with people who come to the group. We could have *known each other in a past life or be in the same soul group.*'

'It sounds like you're a little smitten with him,' answered Debs, who felt a little annoyed.

'Smitten?' asked Sapphire.

'Yes, like you have a crush on him?'

'It isn't like that, as you said, Simon is a professional and I respect his opinions. He's become a close friend because we have so much in common. There's nothing more than that, we're both on the same page. You'll understand that one day when you come across people who resonate with you, spiritual soulmates!'

'If you say so. Can we get on with the reiki now please because I need to be home by four.'

'Yes of course,' replied Sapphire, just lie down and relax. I'll just put this bolster under your knees to make you more comfortable.'

Debs started to listen to the relaxing music. She could hear the sound of waves, and some distant wind chimes. Sapphire placed her hands directly on her head, which made her extremely warm and was incredibly relaxing. After a few minutes Debs began to drift. She was neither awake nor asleep but was vaguely aware of some healing dimension or different reality. *Her body was surrounded by beautiful deep purple, streaked with gold*, while a voice that spoke to her said, 'Your life may appear tough at times but we're teaching you resilience. It won't always be like this but accept it for now. Sapphire's here to help you align to your spiritual path, don't push her away because she understands, relax and let go.'

Forty minutes later, Debs heard Sapphire say, 'ok we've finished now,' as she suddenly became aware of her holding her feet. *The energy felt as if she was connecting to the earth* and Debs didn't know what to say. For a few moments she had no idea where she was. Where did she go and how long had she been lying on the couch in this beautiful cabin?

'Would you like some water, it helps ground you,' asked Sapphire.

'Yes, please, that was incredible. I feel like I've been lying here for hours, what time is it?'

'It's only three forty, so give yourself five minutes to be back and ground.'

Debs felt restored. Oddly, *the reiki felt like a good night's sleep*, and she felt refreshed and somehow different. She no longer cared what Stewie was up to in Scotland, as long as he was having a good time. Any thoughts about him having an affair had completely disappeared. It was ridiculous that she even imagined that when he would never have the time!

'Right, let me pay you,' she said.

'You don't have to pay me Debs, your family,' Sapphire replied, but if you want to put a small donation in the pot, it's over there because I'm saving up for a yoga retreat. I can't expect John to pay for that if I'm going on my own, that's unless you would be interested in coming?'

'Perhaps,' but who would look after the girls?

'Stewie,' replied Sapphire. It would do him good. Here take this, it's *rose quartz*. Put it on your heart chakra when you go to bed. *It's great for emotional healing and unconditional love.* I use one all the time because John and I have a lot to heal.'

'I can imagine,' replied Debs. She held the stone in her hand. It had a warm friendly energy, which was gentle and soft like a loving heart. 'I'll come again soon. Is a month good for you?

'Yes, I'll book you in for a month's time and I'll text you about your appointment, so you'll have it on your phone.'

'Great,' replied Debs, who was glowing and realised that there were more glows than pregnancy, she'd just never been aware of them. She had so, much to learn about spirituality and couldn't wait to discover more!'

Debs arrived home, paid Poppy twenty pounds for her trouble and started to prepare food for herself and the girls. Her phone had been off all afternoon. When she turned it on, there was a text from Stewie to say Scotland was stunning and he was really enjoying himself. Debs felt surprised but happy. He'd sent a few stunning pictures of Loch Lomond and said he'd cruised around the Loch for three hours. The weather looked sunny, and Stewie looked much more like his old self. Debs felt better, in fact, she put away the vegetables she'd taken out of the fridge and decided to order Pizza as a treat. Why not, she was on holiday too! They were having a holiday from each other and that was a good thing because when Stewie returned home, they would see a better version of each other. They needed to get the old magic back now; it had been a long time. Debs didn't want them to turn into a replica of his parents who were moving in different directions. She'd been surprised by Sapphire's feelings for Simon, there was an attraction there, but it felt one sided. She'd obviously *been carried away by this whole soul mate's thing!* She only hoped that didn't happen to her because she wanted Stewie to be in her life and for him to understand her. If she joined the Wednesday group, Stewie would have to babysit the girls but surely that wasn't too much of an ask. The Reiki had been so helpful it intrigued her. Was it something she could learn herself, because it would be useful for her and the girls.

STEWIE AT LOCH LOMOND

Stewie was mesmerised. He'd never experienced such beautiful scenery on a day when the sky was cloud-free, and the sun was beaming down on him. He was a little disappointed that Debs wasn't with him, because enjoying a stunning view was really something, but sharing these moments with someone you care about was special. Surprisingly, Georgia hadn't crossed his mind. He was annoyed that he'd put himself out of his way to try and talk her round when she was having none of it. What a waste of time. The woman obviously didn't care that much about him. She certainly wasn't the person he thought she was, and he regretted his involvement with her because it was messy and had changed things between him and Debs. He was certain that Debs knew nothing of his affair, although she may have picked up something subconsciously because she'd distanced herself for months. She now slept in the spare bedroom, which was a shame when she'd changed so much over the last few weeks, looking slimmer and more sophisticated. He was unsure how to go about reconnecting with her. He'd never felt good enough for her, and with his business worries and his affair, he felt even less about himself. He wished the whole 'Georgia episode' could be washed away because it made him feel guilty, which blocked any kind of intimacy between them. He now felt as if he didn't have either of them, plus his sense of abandonment had escalated in recent weeks until this trip with his father, which had come as a real surprise.

The boat moored against the small dock, and the passengers started to leave, saying thank you to the crew as they left. Stewie had never known a few hours go so quickly. The trip had been amazing, and there was even a bar on the boat for a cold beer!

The loch had been far bigger than he imagined. They didn't travel to the far reaches of it, but it appeared endless. They would still covered quite a distance, and he'd learned a lot about the history of the loch with the aid of a commentary played throughout the boat, which was highly informative. Stewie looked at his mobile and decided to call John to let him know that he'd be back for dinner the incredible smoked salmon and other feasts which their first-class dining room had to offer! He'd heard the mention of caviar while passing, and why not? He may as well try all the delights Scotland had to offer!

'Hi John, I've finished the cruise. It was an incredible experience, as you described. I'll be back shortly for pre-dinner drinks,' said an enthusiastic Stewie.

'And I've had the most incredible round of golf, completing it in record time. Who would have thought I'd achieve my personal best!' John replied enthusiastically.

'Wow, that's great. I'll watch you tomorrow, and you can teach me some tricks. I'm just approaching the club now.'

'Tricks? What tricks! Golf is a game of skill, but you're welcome to come and watch. You can carry my clubs if they're not too heavy for you.'

'Yeah, sure,' replied Stewie, as he wondered what he'd let himself in for. It was such an early start, and he'd thought about having a bit of a lie-in tomorrow, but that wasn't going to happen when Dr John liked keeping on the move!

* * * * *

Sapphire was delighted to have her space back! She'd smudged the whole house with sage and took a long, deep breath as she sat down in her favourite chair—the one John usually occupied! Her work schedule for next week looked busy: four clients a day. Surprisingly, she was now making the same money as she'd earned at the bank and enjoying it twice as much. She'd learned a lot about manifesting recently and setting her intentions. Although she'd discovered it was easy to do this, she'd also become aware that it was impossible to change another person's free will because of universal law. John was stubborn and difficult at times. He was never going to change, but while he was away, at least she had breathing space. She still loved him, but their relationship had become mundane.

Was it wrong to crave excitement when most people were happy and settled by their age or appeared to be? Since her interest in spirituality, she'd learned so much, but wanting to change John had been her greatest challenge. She could hope and pray, but that was about it. She knew she wasn't the woman she was thirty years ago, and that wasn't a bad thing, but it felt lonely at times. She craved spending time with like-minded souls who understood or 'got' her, so she could relax or even laugh. Deep within her soul, she was deeply serious. Had she lost her sense of humour, or had her humour changed? When John chuckled on the sofa over some old television soap or other familiar series, she cringed. It wasn't easy to appear amused when she was so bored, and pretending was fake. Her heart ached with loneliness and lack of companionship.

John suddenly sent a text, and her phone beeped. It said he'd achieved his personal best while playing nine holes. Sapphire couldn't digest what he'd said. She didn't have an answer for something she felt so detached from! She searched in the emojis for a quick solution and sent the smiley one with a single heart. Sapphire then dropped four drops of Rock Rose into her mouth, then decided—sod it—she'd have to make a move on Simon!

SIMON (a week later)

Simon was up to his eyes with client bookings and felt jaded. It was only Wednesday afternoon, so he still had to work another two days this week. Fortunately, he only had one more client to see today, before making something to eat, then going to the group. Debs had texted him to say that she was joining them this week. It was slightly awkward with her being a client, when the group always discussed things on a personal level, but he was used to keeping professionalism when he had to. His last client was called John. He was a doctor, which was always difficult as doctors were notoriously sceptical. He'd said on the phone that he was suffering from addictions, too much alcohol, and cigars but there was also another thing that he'd discuss when he saw him. He wanted help to get on top of these situations because he was not only worried about the drink driving aspect but being a doctor he had his reputation to uphold.

Simon found John to be friendly, polite, and articulate as he expected from a doctor. He shook Simon's hand, and they sat down in two comfortable lounge chairs, which sat opposite each other to have a long chat before the hypnotherapy.

'You said on the phone that you were worried about alcohol and smoking too much. I can help with those, but is there anything else?'

'Yes, there is, but it's embarrassing.' John took a long deep breath, 'I've found myself looking at porn recently. I've no idea why, but late at night after my wife has gone to bed, I've started watching all sorts of rubbish.'

Simon looked at John intensely, nothing surprised him, addictions could manifest in so many different ways. There was often a deep loneliness or need of some sort, which made people do things out of character. It could be anything, drugs, alcohol, porn, smoking, weight problems or an overactive sex drive, the list went on!

John started to talk about his life. He was suffering from boredom and lack of fulfilment, apart from when he played golf, which he always enjoyed. When he talked about his wife, Simon suddenly realised he was discussing Sapphire and John wasn't aware that he attended his wife's meditation group. Simon decided that at this point it was better not to tell him because it could make him feel uncomfortable. John went on to explain that the porn started about two years ago when his wife lost interest in sex. He said they would grow apart, and she rarely spoke to him unless it was about their son, or the grandchildren coming over, which they occasionally did on a Sunday. He said his wife had turned into a *new age hippy* and they no longer had anything in common. He wanted to try and understand her world, but it had proved impossible. If he got *on top of his addictions,* he thought it would help.

Simon spent the next hour meticulously taking notes about what happened over the last few years. He decided that he could work with John as he'd been successful with many cases of addiction. Losing weight was the most popular one but porn was no big thing, as he'd heard it said many times before with working professionals. He wondered how John had found him. Was it purely random, or had Sapphire mentioned him. If this was the case, John wasn't letting on. Perhaps Debs had mentioned her sessions. Simon was aware that he was being pulled into a family web, which was a place he didn't want to go, but unless there was a good reason, he didn't feel he could refuse to help.

Thirty minutes later John opened his eyes. 'I feel great. I could hear you talking to me throughout the session. It will be interesting to find out what happens after I pour myself a whisky.'

'It isn't instantaneous John, but I'm sure our session will help. It will take three or four appointments before you notice any huge changes. We can work on all the addictions at the same time, which will make things quicker. Obviously, you must want to build a bridge with Sapphire for your relationship to improve, it won't just happen because you've kicked the addictions when there are many reasons why the communication has broken down. Sapphire must also want things to change.'

'Unfortunately, Goldilocks hides in her cabin and isn't interested in anything I have to say. It's become a bit of a woman shed. A man's shed I can understand, but this is ridiculous.'

'Why would it be different, man, woman, or transgender shed?' asked Simon.

'Because a man needs to escape from his wife doesn't he, to get away from the continual nagging and boring talk!'

'Interesting,' replied Simon, taking notes.

'So, you would like Sapphire to talk to you more, but not about the things that bore you. What would you like to talk about?'

'Things that I'm interested in, like golf! Or she could ask me how my day went, anything as long as it isn't crystals, past lives, or witchy stuff.'

'I see,' replied Simon.

'I'm glad you do because I don't get any of it, she's driving me to drink.'

'Let's see how it goes. I can book you in for a fortnight?'

'That sounds fine,' replied John, who was amazed at how relaxed he felt.

John walked out into the daylight. *The day appeared brighter than when he arrived! Was it his imagination, or were the grass and trees a brighter colour green?* He heard a blackbird sing its incredible song, which he was surprised by because he hadn't paid attention to bird song for years. That was something he could do, bird watching. He'd loved going in the past. He may even ask Sapphire if she'd like to come, they had two pairs of binoculars. He turned on the car radio and heard Lady in Red playing, which was the first song they danced to, thirty years ago. He found it incredible, undoubtedly a coincidence, and it took him back. He'd never really liked the song, but Sapphire had, and it was played frequently at the time. The good old days when they used to cosy up together on the sofa. Could they ever be like that again, he doubted it.

When John arrived home at four, Sapphire was sitting in the lounge reading. 'What's that about?' he asked.

'It's an astrology book,' Sapphire replied, then smiled. 'Where have you been? I thought we were going to look for curtains, but I couldn't find you anywhere.'

'Well, I usually can't find you, because you're always in that cabin.'

'I'm not in the cabin now, am I? I'll put the kettle on, tea? You're acting very mysteriously, where have you been?' she repeated.

'Oh, just a therapy session. I'll tell you about it if it works. I'm going back for a few more. I'm stressed, so I thought it might help.'

'Ah ok, we can always do curtains another time. You haven't told me about how you and Stewie got on over the weekend in Scotland.'

'I text you about it and you know I don't like doing that,' John replied.

'I know that you text me, but have you made any progress with the business thing?' replied Sapphire feeling frustrated.

'I've given him some money, which he's going to use to promote his business. He's also thinking about going into partnership with someone who has been working in recruitment for twenty odd years and is remarkably successful.'

'That sounds like a good plan. Did he enjoy the golf?"

'He didn't play. He watched for a while and then went out for day trips around Glasgow, I'm surprised he hasn't told you. He went on a boat trip around the Loch, which I knew he'd enjoy. He's thinking about taking Debs next year if we can look after the girls.'

'Ah yes, nice, although Debs might come on a yoga retreat with me next year.'

'A yoga retreat sounds a bit insular.'

'Insular, I could say golf is bloody insular. You always go on your own and you're gone for hours.'

John sat down on a chair opposite and began to drink his tea. What was Sapphire's objection to golf? He'd always thought that she didn't mind. It was his hobby, and he certainly wasn't going to change that.

'I've been thinking about bird watching. Would you like to come with me on my day off next week?'

'Bird watching. Well, it's not really my thing, is it?'

'What is your thing, Sapphire? Reading all this woo-woo stuff and when I try to spend any time with you, you don't want to know.'

'I'm sorry. I promise I'll think about it. Anyway, I've got to get set up for this evening, dinner is cooking in the oven, and I need to get the cabin prepared.'

John got up from his chair to grab the newspaper. He wanted to sit in the conservatory, which had already become his shed. He'd reappear at six when dinner was ready. At least he'd tried suggesting something to Sapphire, but she wouldn't play ball. This hypnotherapy thing could be a waste of time. He went to pour himself a small whisky. It was his day off, so, why not. As he took a sip, he noticed that it tasted quite different. 'Cat's piss,' he shouted, running to the kitchen sink to spit it out. What the hell happened?'

* * * * *

It was six pm and the dinner smelt delicious. John heard Sapphire dishing up. He recognised the aroma of a beef casserole of some kind, stroganoff, or something similar. Sapphire was an exceedingly good cook and despite what she got up to in the cabin, she always had dinner ready on time.

Sapphire knew her friends would arrive at around six fifty so there wasn't much time to eat. While she dished up, John hovered around her in the kitchen. She wasn't eating beef anyway and had made herself a light salad, which she took out of the fridge.

'Shall I pour a glass of wine?' John asked.

'Not for me, because I'm teaching meditation at seven but don't let me stop you.'

'Maybe I'll save that nice red until Saturday evening because I'm trying to cut down on alcohol, in fact I just had a pre-dinner whisky, and it didn't taste the same. It must have been a bad bottle or something! We can share the red on Monday after the bird watching. We'll order in a takeaway or there's a new Indian Restaurant in the town that I heard deliver.'

'Are we bird watching then? I don't remember agreeing to that or saying that I wanted to go. I don't mind going another Monday, but this Monday I'm going on a one-day yoga retreat, and I won't be back until after five.'

'Next Sunday then? Oh no, I've got golf.'

Sapphire finished dishing up and walked into the dining room with the plates. 'We can go another weekend if you really want to. It isn't something I'm interested in, but I don't mind going once to try it. Are you losing the taste for alcohol, which would be good because we spend a lot on drink.'

'I'm definitely losing the taste for something,' John said with a grin.

'You know I love you, it's just that things have changed,' Sapphire explained.

'You mean you've changed. Since you left the bank and started all this healing stuff. I sometimes wonder if I'm married to a different person. Look at you, you even look different.'

'Is that a bad thing, people evolve and change. You can't expect everything to stay the same as thirty years ago.'

'Talking of thirty years ago, that song you loved was played on the car radio. 'Lady in Red,' remember, the one we had our first dance too. I couldn't help but smile.'

'It reminds me of Diana.'

'What, it doesn't remind you of us?'

'No, not really. It was years ago, why would it?'

John walked out of the dining room in search of the special red. He filled up his glass. He was in total disbelief. She wasn't the same woman he'd married; she'd been replaced by an alien! 'Fuck her,' he thought if something didn't change soon, he couldn't be responsible for what he'd do. He walked back into the dining room and noticed that Sapphire's plate had already gone. No doubt it had been put in the dishwasher already, and she'd gone to start her development circle, or whatever she called it.

John finished eating his meal and practically knocked back a whole glass of red before pouring another. 'Drowning in red,' he thought whimsically, it tasted far better than the whisky he'd tried earlier! He looked out of the window and noticed a good-looking man in his early forties, tall with dark hair, enter through the side gate and walk across to the cabin. Hang on a minute, wasn't that Simon the hypnotherapist? Yes, it certainly looked like him. He felt angry for a moment. Simon and the others were having his wife's full attention when he couldn't even manage to have a decent meal with her. He staggered into the conservatory and openly started watching porn. Why didn't he say anything? It made him look like a fool. All that stuff he'd shared about Sapphire, and he likely knew most of it! He wondered if there was anything going on between them, then thought it doubtful, because he wouldn't fancy a woman of Sapphire's age. Besides, she was far too loyal to encourage him; however, he couldn't be certain. Was this why she wasn't interested in having sex with him, she had a crush on the hypnotherapist? Mind you, a crush was all it would be, because he felt that deep down Sapphire loved him and there was no way she'd be unfaithful. Not that sort of a woman, he thought, turning to the screen. 'Oh my God,' he muttered as he became transfixed. His addictions had started to run high and, even though the taste of whisky had changed, his other tastes were way out of control.

* * * * * *

Sapphire turned on some relaxing music and made sure everyone was comfortably seated. Surprisingly, Debs had joined them this week, so there was Debs, Simon and four other regulars. Two were retired women who lived locally, who had joined them a few months ago. One was a younger male; a friend of Simons, and Debs had brought a work friend, a teacher at the primary school. Sapphire was pleased that there were now seven members of the group because it was a good number. She started with an easy meditation where they went for a walk through the forest, sat under a tree, and connected with the energy of the tree to bring back any messages or insights from the forest. After about fifteen minutes, Sapphire started the journey back and asked the group to wiggle their fingers and toes, open their eyes and be back in the room. The two older ladies said they enjoyed the experience, they felt extremely relaxed, but didn't hear anything from the tree spirits.

Debs suddenly said, 'I heard something,' and Sapphire encouraged her to share her experience with the group.

'There was a sound like a heartbeat, but it didn't feel as if it was mine. I felt as if the tree and I had become one, and it was whispering to me.

'What did it say?' Sapphire asked, encouragingly. Debs became aware that the group were focused on her as if she was going to make some big revelation and she wanted to run and hide. Had she embarrassed herself?

'I could hear the words, it's time. The tree's energy felt like an old grandfather. For some reason, I kept thinking grandfather time,' explained Debs who felt her voice wavering.

'Grandfather time, how interesting' answered Simon.

'It's meant to be a paradox,' explained Sapphire. The fact the tree spoke to you with this message was strange because it's about time travel but it's also saying that you can't change the past, anyone else?'

Simon then said *he felt very connected to the tree*. He felt the tree's energy was running right through him from the roots to his feet, and then up through his chakras to his crown. He felt taller and stronger like *he recognised the spirit of the tree*, but he'd forgotten it. He also ventured into a *past life* where he was a native American Indian, where some of the trees were sacred and they weren't allowed to touch them unless there was a ceremony. He saw a young woman in his vision with a baby. He knew that he loved her, and felt she was his wife. There were a group of women weaving a blanket and they also took turns to carry the baby.'

Sapphire hadn't been on the journey because she had to keep an eye on everyone to make sure they were safe and had to be ready to bring them out of the meditation quickly if anyone became distressed.

Simon smiled at Debs. For some reason he saw her in a new light. Not this timid scared woman who did everything to please everyone, but as a small supportive woman who was a great teacher, and a good mother to her children. Had it been her in the meditation? Her eyes looked the same, they had a beautiful gentleness about them, which made you feel safe and supported. This is crazy, Simon thought, he had no interest in Debs, first, she was a client, and second, she was married. He tried to rid himself of the image of her eyes and decided that he would offer to pour some water for the group.

Sapphire noticed that for some reason Simon appeared interested in Debs. Something had happened during the *meditation*, but what? Did Debs also have a *past life* with him? They appeared deeply *connected on a soul level*. There was only ten minutes left of the session, so they began sharing their thoughts and feelings about various topics, and Sapphire read some information relating to the chakras.

The members then started to put their coats on to leave. Simon was the last one to go, being polite and holding the door open for the others. Sapphire smiled at him. She was still experiencing a pang of jealousy about Debs, but she didn't know why, it was irrational.

'Thank you for being here, Simon,' she said as she ran her hand down the side of his face and touched his hair.

'What are you doing? You know it isn't like that between us. *We have a connection* but that's it. *You can have many connections with people as you start to awaken,*' Simon explained feeling agitated.

'But *you and I have shared past lives together*, you know that because we've talked about it many times in the group. We have more than friendship between us.

'Sapphire, I come to this group because I want to learn. I respect you as a teacher, but I don't understand where all this is coming from. I want to feel comfortable here, but I'm not sure if I do. I can sense something different about you, what's going on? Has something happened between you and John. Have things got worse?'

'No, things haven't got worse; in fact, he asked me to go birdwatching with him today.'

'Birdwatching that's great. Why don't you go then? If you do some things together it could improve things.'

'I don't need marriage advice from you Simon, besides, you've never been married so you wouldn't know what it's like, day in day out, every day the same. Feeling lonely because you can't even have a conversation.'

'Sapphire, I'm sorry, but I must go. I had no idea that you felt like this but if you do have feelings towards me, I need to move on because this isn't what I want, and it will only make thing's awkward between us.'

'It didn't stop you looking at Debs though. I saw you gazing into her eyes after the meditation, she transfixed you, and you've only recently met. Well, no, not just met, because she told me that she's been seeing you for therapy.'

'Yes, she is, but that's her business, not yours. I never discuss my clients with others, you know that.

'Ok, fuck off then. Don't come back to my group. I don't need you here, especially if you are going to keep staring at my daughter-in-law.'

Simon was fuming, but he knew better than to say anything else, he'd learned that a long time ago. No doubt Sapphire would regret what she said and send a text to apologise in the morning.

'Ok then, if you change your mind, text me.'

'I won't,' she said, 'I'm going inside now, goodnight.'

Sapphire hurried across the grass. It was dark now, and she followed the path alongside the swimming pool to go through the conservatory door, which she seldom did, but she wanted to get inside as quickly as possible. As she walked in, she noticed John had fallen to sleep in the chair with a half empty bottle of red next to him. The sound from the television surprised her, what had he been watching? Sapphire sat down on one of the chairs, and for a few minutes, she was transfixed, which quickly turned into rage! She turned off the television with such vigour the set rocked on its stand.

'What the hell,' she shouted. Could things get any worse? She'd been certain Simon had feelings for her, and he'd dismissed her like she was no-one to him. She grabbed the bottle of red from the side and walked into the kitchen to pour herself a glass. It was ages since she'd drunk, but it felt like the obvious solution to calm her out of control feelings.

Her phone beeped and there was a message from Debs, which said, thanks for inviting me to the group Sapphire, I really enjoyed it. What a great group of people, and it was so interesting.

'Yes, it was great, wasn't it? I'm glad you enjoyed meeting the group. Unfortunately, Simon won't be coming back because he has another commitment.

'Really, that's a shame but fair enough, I'll be there next week. Anyway, see you Sunday.'

Sapphire went to bed in the spare room. There was no way she wanted to sleep next to that boozy porn infested man! Tomorrow morning, she'll cleanse the house with sage again then start a detox. Bird watching was no longer an option, as if that would fix anything!

BEN GETS IN TOUCH

Debs mobile buzzed. It was late Monday afternoon, and she'd just returned from the school and nursery run. She was astounded to see Ben's number pop up because she hadn't spoken to him for months.

'Hello Sis, I haven't heard from you for ages. I thought I'd give you a call to see what's new in your life. I know I live in Glasgow, but it isn't on the other side of the world. We should try and connect more, even if it's voice message.'

'Hi Ben, it's been ages. How are you? Last time we spoke was in the Spring when you were going to Japan, since then, I've not heard from you, everything ok?'

'I'm good thanks, I just wanted to catch up with my little sis to see how things were going with you and the girls, plus Stewie of course. I wondered what you were doing at Christmas because I've got a fortnight off work, so I was thinking about taking the train or driving down to see you. It's that time of year, which reminds me of Mum and Dad. I can't believe it's been over five years now, sometimes it feels like yesterday.'

Debs remembered what a sensitive soul Ben was, and how losing their parents had hit him hard. He was living in Glasgow at the time; he stayed on after finishing university and now worked as a teacher in adult education.

'I miss you Ben,' she said suddenly.

'The girls are fine. It's just Stewie and I, his business has been really struggling since covid, and now there's a wall between us. I know it's hard for him, but it isn't easy for me either, with work or looking after the girls. It's a full-time job; there isn't much time for fun.'

'No dancing, like you used to, then?' he asked.

'No, ballroom went out of the window, Stewie wasn't interested. We went for a few weeks earlier this year, but as he works late, we couldn't commit to it. I'd have continued on my own but then we would have needed a sitter for the girls. Poppy doesn't mind coming over sometimes, but she doesn't want to do evenings.'

'Oh Debs, everyone needs fun, don't they? I'll have to come down and take you out. Stewie can babysit. Sounds like you need a bit of support from your older brother.'

'That would be good, and of course you can come for Christmas. We still have a spare bedroom as the girls are in bunkbeds in the second room. Let me know the dates and I can let Stewie know later, make sure he's around. Talking about support, I've been going for a little hypnotherapy recently. I've had three sessions now, just confidence stuff, and a bit about Mum and Dad. I'm feeling much better than I did, it's been great. Simon, the therapist, goes to Sapphire's group. I've got so much to tell you, so many things have happened since we last spoke. I've started to feel like a different person. I'll save it until you come because it's a lot on the phone.'

'I can't wait. I should be able to come but it could be Christmas Eve, I'll confirm. It will be great Debs. I'm looking forward to it already. I bet the girls have changed.'

'They certainly have; they seem to change weekly. Elsbeth is developing a mind of her own. She's changed a lot since starting school.'

'Like you then, strong minded. Mind you, despite being stubborn, *you were always their favourite,*' said Ben.

'I was their *favourite*?'

'Yeah, you know you were. Dad put you first all the time, they never stopped talking about you, because you were the youngest.'

'That's strange because I never saw it that way. We do have a lot to talk about Ben; I'm really looking forward to seeing you.'

The call finished and Debs was astounded. She was the favourite, really, she would never have guessed it. It had never felt like that. Obviously, *each child had a different perspective* according to their position in the family. She quickly brushed it aside because *the therapy had taught her not to hold onto things, the way she used to*. It was what it was. At the end of the day, did it matter? Sadly, her parents were gone, and no doubt they did their best. There was no point in blaming them for anything. Now she was a parent herself, she knew how hard it was! She tried not to have any favouritism between Elsbeth and Florence. They were both her children, and her love for them was the same. Stewie was also good with both of them; favourites didn't come into it. It was easy to feel *insecure about things from your childhood, but they weren't always real. Another illusion* she thought, *but since she had started to let go, and put herself first, her life had come into focus.* Yes, she would go out with Ben when he came down at Christmas, and she also wanted to rejoin the ballroom and Latin dance class because no doubt there would be some available male to dance with, or she could ask a friend. If Stewie wasn't going to be around for her, she'd have to make her own life, with or without children. *Her self-denial had become a thing of the past. and she had to make life happen!*

PRE-CHRISTMAS VISIT

Stewie felt happier because his recent business promotions had started to pay off. He now had more vacancies to fill because some large companies had chosen to use him, and he had signed contracts with them, which ran for twelve months. If he could provide the staff they needed, then they promised to extend it. This was great because it enabled him to get out of the debt that he'd created during covid. He was interviewing new candidates most of the time. Although his time was precious, he'd recently decided to leave the office at six, so he could spend more time with Debs, and the girls before the children went to bed.

Stewie was grateful for John helping him out. His investment had made a huge difference, and he made sure John knew that he'd been able to turn things around. It was always difficult this time of year, but it felt as if there wouldn't be a Christmas lull this year because his recruitment campaigns extended into the new year and beyond. Having his *father's approval, had also made a huge difference to Stewie because it made him feel more secure* and finally this whole 'train as a doctor thing was behind them. John may never be that interested in his business, but his financial support had helped their relationship to take a turn for the better. They were having lunch with John and Sapphire today and the children were excited. The school term was over, and it was now the day before Christmas Eve. Debs appeared incredibly stressed during the last few days of term because end of terms were always challenging but she was excited about her brother coming to stay. Ben was arriving tomorrow and addition to everything else, she'd been cleaning the house. Sheets were hanging up everywhere to dry because she was reluctant to use the tumble dryer due to soaring electricity costs. The weather was cold and damp, and the girls were disappointed that they couldn't swim in their grandparents' pool this time of year. Hats, gloves, scarves, and wellies had to be found for winter walks, in case Sapphire felt energetic and wanted to take them out. She normally did, because Sapphire had loads of energy and was always enthusiastic about spending time with the girls. Even if it was dark, they would walk around the village and see all the Christmas lights.

The energy and excitement of Christmas was well in the air and Stewie decided that enough was enough and that he was taking holiday from when he left off on Christmas Eve, until after New Year. He'd informed most of his customers already, and as no-one was doing any recruitment over the Christmas holidays, it made sense. He hadn't heard a thing from Georgia, but at the back of his mind he thought about meeting up for a Christmas drink and decided to message her. He'd suggest meeting as 'friends' to find out where he was with her, and if friendship was possible. He didn't know why he wanted to see her, when things had improved between him and Debs, at least there was some physical contact now. It was hard to admit, but this guy Simon was working some kind of magic, because she seemed a lot more cheerful. Her stress levels didn't appear to be as bad as before, and she was looking great. Her waist was thinner and her stomach flatter, and when she wore jeans, he couldn't help but feel some of the desire he had when they first met! Debs looked hot, so why did he have this urge to meet Georgia, that's if she wanted to speak to him, as she hadn't answered any of his texts. Why did the unavailable always appear so attractive? Did he just enjoy the thrill of the chase? He knew that deep down he loved Debs, but her conversation always revolved around how the children were getting on at school, which bored him. She occasionally mentioned something from her woo-woo books, but he wasn't interested in them either, so why bother when she could share that with Sapphire. *'Staying present,'* what was that all about? Surely, *he was always present*, where else would he be? His head was never stuck in the past, apart from when he thought about his physical relationship with Georgia, which tended to be when he was driving. He didn't have time to think about her while he was working, or when the girls were screaming over some toy, they both wanted to play with!

Hats, coats, and gloves were on, and the girls were now sitting in the car saying they were hot! Stewie turned down the car heater. He was surprised how many houses had a huge Santa or snowman in the garden. The number of lights these gardens had was crazy. He thought there was an energy crisis, but he'd still put on the tumble drier when they got home because he was sick of looking at the laundry hanging around the house. It couldn't cost that much, and they had to tidy up before Ben came.

They finally reached Beaumont Cottage at 1 pm. The girls were hungry, and Sapphire said lunch would be ready for them and it was. As soon as they entered the house there seemed to be a strange vibe between Sapphire and John. It was as if Sapphire was putting on a happy show but could burst into tears at any moment.

'Is everything ok?' Stewie asked John, giving him a smile.

'Yes, of course son. How's business, I hope it's continuing to pick up?'

'I'm still busy, Dad, and I'm on holiday from the end of tomorrow until New Year, as usual, and there isn't any recruiting over Christmas.

I have some great new contracts going forward for twelve months minimum.'

'Wow, that's great news. I knew you'd get through, just needed a little encouragement,' replied John.

'Yes well, I'm getting there now.'

'Is Debs happy?' asked John. 'She looks slimmer.'

'Yeah, she's been seeing some hypnotherapist guy. He seems to have brought out the magic in her for some reason.'

'That would be Simon. I've seen him a couple of times, but I'm not entirely sure about him. After our session, my whisky tasted like cats' piss, and I haven't been able to drink it since. I know I said I wanted to cut down, but I wasn't expecting that!'

Stewie laughed, 'cat's piss, I should go; it sounds interesting. The roast looks good, shall we eat?'

They sat down and the girls started chatting to their grandma about school, while Stewie and John were deep in conversation about business plans, which pleased Debs. She noticed there was definitely something amiss with Sapphire who hadn't looked in John's direction once. She collected their plates and left his and he sheepishly stood up to take his own plate into the kitchen.

'Come on Sapphire,' Debs heard him say. You're making a fuss about nothing.'

'Am I? You wonder why I spend all my time in the cabin, well, it's to get away from you.'

'Shh, keep your voice down. We don't want to upset the family. We can have a proper chat later; can you please try? It's Christmas!'

Sapphire went to the bathroom and sprayed herself with angelic aura spray. She wanted to get rid of John's energy. It was vile. She'd make the best of the situation because she didn't want to spoil the family's pre-Christmas meal, but she had to get away, take a break from here. Her stomach was turning over and over, and she had little appetite. There hadn't been a word from Simon. He obviously wasn't returning to the group. *I guess it's because I told him to 'fuck off,'* she thought, had she gone in a little heavy! What had come over her. She hadn't felt jealous of anyone for years, but when she saw that look between him and Debs, she lost control. There was only one way forward, and that was to meditate, rebalance and let him go. If he was meant for her, he'd be back.

'What is meant for you never passes you by,' what kind of stupid expression was that? She'd got it from somewhere. The question was, what shall I do while I wait for that thing, which never passes me by? She'd spent enough years passing by already with John and now look at him. He wasn't the man she married. He was some out of sync weirdo whose bad habits were getting out of control, and he thought she was embarrassing!

'What on earth's up with you two?' asked Debs when Sapphire returned to the table. John had excused himself and gone to the conservatory, while Sapphire started dishing up the girl's too much ice cream, which brought big smiles to their faces.

'Whoa, that's way too much, they're not adults,' exclaimed Debs.

'It needs to be used up, or it will go in the bin. John doesn't eat desserts and I'm on a diet.'

'What you, on a diet. You don't need to lose weight, you're perfect.'

'I can't go into it all now, Debs. All I can say is that John isn't behaving like the John I know and love, things have become a little sticky between us.'

'It's sticky,' shouted Florence whose ice cream had run down her spoon all over her hand.

Sapphire and Debs looked at each other and laughed. I'll talk to you about it when you come for reiki. Are you going to carry on going for hypnotherapy?' asked Sapphire.

'Yes, I told you that, it really helped. I feel far more confident since we worked on the feelings I had about my parents.'

'Perhaps I should go,' Sapphire remarked.

'I thought you couldn't wait to see the back of him?' replied Debs.

'You are right. I didn't want him in the group because it felt like he was taking over but it doesn't mean that I don't admire what he does. I'm sure John went to see him. I knew he'd gone to see a therapist for addictions, but I didn't realise it was Simon until he mentioned where he lived. He's getting a lot of business from this family!'

'I'd like to train in hypnotherapy. Simon thinks I'd be good at it,' declared Debs, who then realised that letting the cat out of the bag wasn't one of her best ideas.

Stewie, who had been messaging on his mobile, taking little notice of their conversation, suddenly looked up. 'What you, learn something like that.

You're exhausted doing part time teaching, I don't know how you'll fit that in.'

'Neither do I, but where there's a will there's a way! Isn't that right, Sapphire.'

'Yeah, for sure,' she replied.

Sapphire felt irritated that Simon had been discussing hypnotherapy with Debs, when she could have been developing the closeness, she had with him. The world was so unfair. She didn't know how to begin repairing her friendship with Simon. For now, it seemed best not to contact him about the group, and to wait and see *if their paths crossed in the future*, which was likely because they were *walking in a similar direction*. It still left this horrible energy between her and John, perhaps if she agreed to this bird-watching thing, it would be a distraction. They could go when the weather was a little better because it would definitely be too cold over Christmas.

Life without John would be difficult because he'd always *been her rock,* but lately she'd become so insecure. The group brought her security, and she loved teaching, but she now wondered if their meetups had been more about the prospect of seeing Simon than teaching, which wasn't her intention. She could feel *her neediness* and wanted to kick herself. This *empty feeling* had become worse. She felt better if she kept herself busy playing with her grandchildren, but apart from those odd few hours, it was constantly there. *She felt abandoned* and it niggled her to hear about Debs enthusiasm to add another string to her bow when her own bow felt broken. She'd carry on with the group but somehow it wouldn't be the same, all because of *her jealousy*. *Sabotage* thought Sapphire, just as things were beginning to take off. It was time to learn something new. She'd thought about the yoga training, but it was a big expense and the course was intensive. It was for a month, and she'd have to travel, or there was a slightly shorter course, which was also residential. 'Sod it, I'll book the long one,' she thought. At least I'll get away and think about the direction my life is taking.

'UNO, it is then. I'll put the dishes in the dishwasher and you two can get the games out. Just let me wipe the table down first and please go and wash your hands straight away because we can't have sticky ice cream all over the cards,' said Sapphire, who had perked up.

'I'll go and see what John's up to,' suggested Stewie as he strode towards the conservatory.'

'Probably porn,' replied Sapphire.

'Stewie, turned around in total disbelief. 'Surely it's not that bad,' he replied.

'Yes, it is,' she said, as she began shuffling the cards.

CHRISTMAS EVE

Debs felt relieved that school was over. At least for now, but she'd still have to prepare some work during the two-week break. Stewie's mobile alarm buzzed, and he reluctantly climbed out of bed to get showered. 'Aren't you getting up?' he asked.

'No, it's Christmas Eve, so, I'm staying right here in this warm cosy bed. Ben will be here late afternoon. What a long drive but he seems keen to come. Please be quiet going past the girls' room, because they are asleep and they don't need to wake up yet.'

'Yeah, ok, it's all right for some. I'll see you later then,' he said adjusting his tie while heading for the door. He then shouted back, 'do you want me to bring anything for tonight?'

'A couple of bottles of white if that's ok. We're having curry. I'll make a mild one for the girls. It will be veggie and shh,' replied Debs as she pulled up the covers.

'Oh great, it looks like frost, or a light layer of snow,' he said, peeping out of the bedroom curtains.

'Can you please go? I want to go back to sleep!'

'See you later,' Stewie repeated in a slightly sarcastic tone, as he stomped down the stairs.

Men, thought Debs, why can't they be a little more sensitive, surely, he knows how desperate I am for a lay in. She noticed Stewie had accidentally left his phone on the bedside table. She'd call him on the work phone later. There was no way she was going to get out of this warm bed to try and catch him. She picked up the phone and noticed there was an open text. The screen wasn't locked, and she couldn't help but touch it to see what it said.

'Hi Stewie, I'll meet you after work for a quick drink and catch up, but I haven't got long.' Georgia x.

Georgia thought Debs, she'd never heard Stewie mention her. She could be a work colleague but meeting her on Christmas Eve when Ben was coming? Debs felt guilty for looking at his phone and quickly put it down. She wouldn't ask him about her because he was allowed friends. It just seemed a little odd and *her intuition was flagging it up*. She had seldom experienced this so, strongly, but Sapphire often talked about it, claiming that if you get a *strong feeling about something, then you're usually right*, and this was definitely that!

Debs peeped in on the girls. Surprisingly, they were still asleep, and it was now nine thirty, so she went downstairs to make herself some porridge, and get the cereals out. They were very keen on Weetabix right now. She turned on the kettle and made herself a cup of tea. This was the life, she thought, having time to be more leisurely! She'd make the curry a little later. There were also beds to change. The list was endless with a young family but at least there wasn't that early morning rush when the girls couldn't find a glove, or their reading book went missing! She decided to give them another half an hour before waking them up. Out of the row of cookery books, which sat on a high shelf in the kitchen, Debs selected a great one on vegetarian and vegan curries and soon became absorbed. Her phone buzzed and Ben had sent a text to say that he'd already left and see you soon. Her phone went again and there was a text from Simon.

'Happy Christmas dear Debs, hoping that 2025 brings you all the success and magic you deserve.' Love Simon. There was no kiss which Debs was slightly relieved about. Simon was an extremely attractive man, but he had to be kept in the friend's zone, especially if she was going to do the hypnotherapy training with him, which started in February. Debs was well aware of what happened when Sapphire became attached to him and now John and her were hardly speaking. There was definitely something serious going on there. Despite Stewie being a little distant at times, she loved him and now his business had picked up, there was definite progress. He was trying at least, and she'd noticed he was more affectionate. She'd give him a call about his phone shortly, but she doubted he'd pop back, because he was coming home early, and had already read the text before he left. She decided it was best not to mention it, or it would look like she was suspicious. They didn't need that when they were trying to repair things.

Debs decided to send a Happy Christmas to Simon with a flashing picture of a Christmas tree, which she'd been receiving from her friends. Underneath she wrote, 'thanks Simon, Happy Christmas to you also. See you in the New Year when we can talk about the training. I can't wait Debs x.'

Debs then took the kiss on and off again about five times before deciding to leave it, after all it was Christmas. She heard the girls were up and went up to see if they were all right. They wanted to come down and eat their breakfast in their pyjamas and seeing as she herself wasn't dressed, it would have been unfair to insist otherwise. They were much more relaxed not having to rush off to school. She'd turn on the television and see if there were any decent holiday programs on, then she'd start chopping vegetables and wait for Ben. No doubt he'd be here before Stewie. Is it too early for drinking she wondered, then decided to help herself to a glass of white. It was definitely early in the day to be drinking but she was cooking, and it was holiday time.

'Are we going swimming?' asked Elsbeth.

'No not today. It's too cold and we are having a day in. Your uncle's coming later, you haven't seen him since you were small.

'What's his name?' asked Florence.

'Ben,' replied Debs.

'Like Big Ben? We are learning about that at school,' said Elsbeth.

'Call him Big Ben if you like. He's very tall,' replied Debs.

'We can draw him a line,' said Elsbeth.

'Yes, you can, but you probably won't be able to reach that high.'

The girls were quiet all day. They seemed happy to be at home after a hectic end of term, even Florence was pretty quiet which made a change, which meant Debs was able to get on with some Christmas cooking, mince pies, and a dessert for after the curry. She'd saved some cooking apples, so it was quite easy to turn them into a crumble, which the girls loved.

After what felt like hours of cooking in the kitchen, Debs went to see what the girls were up to and noticed Florence had fallen to sleep on the sofa while Elsbeth was watching a cartoon. She felt a little guilty about not giving them attention, but they seemed fine and when Ben got there, she knew he'd spoil them.

It was now three pm, and it wouldn't be long until Ben arrived. She quickly tidied the kitchen and made sure everything looked orderly for her brother. It had been so long. He'd visited this house, but the girls wouldn't remember, they were so tiny then. A car drew up and Debs heard the crunch of stones on the driveway, then she heard a key in the latch and realised it must be Stewie, not Ben.

'Hi Debs,' he said, bending down to give her a quick kiss on the cheek. I thought I'd come home early to see if you needed any help, I got the wine. What time's Ben coming?'

'Around four, oh hang on there's a text to say that he will be nearer five now. It's such a long drive. It's good of him to come all this way.'

'I know it's a long drive because I did it not long ago. Even though John was driving, it still felt like it took forever. Shall I put the hoover around?'

Debs smiled, she felt relieved that Stewie was being helpful and she'd forgotten about his mobile phone.

'I didn't have time to hoover the bedrooms Stewie, so if you don't mind, that would be really helpful.'

Stewie lifted the hoover upstairs, then remembered his mobile phone was in his bedroom. He walked over to the bed and saw it on his bedside table. He wondered if Debs had read his message from Georgia. She was happy to meet him, which was great but what would he say? Ben would be here too, which made it even more awkward. She was a work colleague, was no doubt the easiest. He changed into his familiar blue jeans and put on a navy sweater. He kept his shirt underneath. He wanted to stay warm this time of year. He then plugged in the hoover and started to clean. He was annoyed at himself for leaving his phone behind. He realised it was missing but he couldn't be bothered to drive home and get it when he was having a short day. At least he'd finished work now and wouldn't be returning until after New Year. It felt like a proper break and about time too.

The sound of the hoover died away and Debs heard Stewie put it back in the downstairs cupboard.

'All done, but you could have told me that I'd forgotten my mobile, Debs. I was looking all over the place for it!'

'Sorry, I remembered first thing, then it went out of my head with Ben coming. I thought you'd come home at lunchtime because you said you were finishing early. You had a text.'

'Did you read it?' asked Stewie.

'Yes, I did, because you'd left it behind and I thought it might be important. Are you really going out to meet someone on Christmas Eve when we have family staying, plus it's snowing!'

'It's only a quick drink. I'll pop out straight after dinner and let you catch up with your brother. We were going to meet straight after work, but then I remembered about Ben, and decided to come home early!'

'Well, go if you want to, but if you're gone for more than a couple of hours, we'll lock the door and you'll have to come down the chimney!' joked Debs, trying to lighten things a little. *She was pretending she didn't mind when she did.* It was their time. Family time and Stewie said that he was finished for Christmas when he clearly hadn't.'

The doorbell chimed. It was Big Ben, and Florence immediately started to stir, while Elsbeth ran as fast as she could to the front door to open it, 'Uncle Ben, Uncle Ben, she shouted.

'Bunkle N,' repeated Florence, who was screaming with excitement, despite the fact she'd just woken up!

Debs hurried to the door, only to see Ben loaded with two large bags of presents. 'I'll just pop back for my case,' he said with a smile. 'It's just started to snow again. We'll have a white Christmas this year!'

'Can make a snowman?' asked Elsbeth.

Ben's bags stood in the hallway, and he quickly shut the front door to give Debs a long hug. 'I needed that,' she said.

'The girls have grown. They've practically doubled in size since I last saw them. Where shall I put the presents?'

'Under the tree please, if you can get over there!' replied Debs.

'Look at the wall, that's how much I've grown. Mummy will have to measure you because I can't reach,' demanded Elsbeth.

'Girls, give Uncle Ben a chance to take his shoes off and have a cup of tea. Sorry Ben, they've been so. excited about you coming and they don't stop. Let's put the kettle on.'

'I'd rather have a whisky please, and maybe a cup of tea later. It was one hell of a journey; I thought I'd never get here.'

'A whisky, I think I'll join you and you can tell me about what you've been up to, but you better have your line drawn first, or the girls will never leave you alone,' suggested Stewie who appeared to have perked up a little with having some male company.

'Ah little monsters,' Ben replied, growling at the girls. 'I'll read them some great monster stories later, and they'll be out like a light.'

Debs poured herself a brandy, added a little ginger and started to relax. It was Christmas, well it was Christmas Eve, near enough. Ben smiled at her, Stewie and Ben were deep in conversation about the journey, the girls were looking at some story books Ben had brought with him, and everything felt well and peaceful. Debs went to draw the curtains, even though it was dark, the moonlight shone on the lawn, and she noticed some large snowflakes had settled. They had shopping in and weren't going anywhere, at least the girls, Ben and she weren't but she wasn't sure about Stewie. Whatever this meetup was about, it was obviously important to him, and why shouldn't he meet up with his colleague for a quick drink? *So, why did her intuition say, 'red flag,'* despite this, she was too scared to delve any deeper!

'Ok, I've got to nip out for a couple of hours, but I won't be long. I hope you don't think I'm rude, but I need to catch up with a work colleague who is having a difficult time.'

'Oh, no worries. I hope she's not on her own for Christmas. You could invite her here if you like?' suggested Debs.

'No, I wouldn't do that, I think she's going to her parents or something?' Stewie felt very awkward and grabbed his car keys saying, 'back soon,' then rushed out of the door.

'See you later,' shouted Ben, but Stewie had already left.

After the girls were ready for bed, she heard Ben telling them a story about a monster who lived in a castle. 'He'd been there for hundreds of years,' he said. All the local people knew about him, but he was lonely.'

Debs hoped that Ben wasn't frightening them out of their wits! She quickly packed the dishwasher, wishing Stewie had helped her before he left, but he was more interested in taking a shower and putting on a new Christmas shirt that his parents gave him! He'd ripped open the packaging, declaring it was Christmas, and why not because nothing else was clean and he wasn't going out looking like Bob the Builder! As Debs walked down the hallway to peep out of the front door to see if the car had started, she suddenly smelt a trail of aftershave, that she didn't recognise. Did Stewie have another life that she knew nothing about? For a few moments she felt devastated because they had been getting on so much better over the last few weeks. He'd been arriving home from work in good time, and they would even started to have kisses and cuddles in bed. It wasn't sex, but they were showing each other affection, which she thought was a good sign. They certainly weren't as close as they were when they first met, but things had started to shift.

With Stewie gone, Debs had the opportunity to chat on her own with Ben, which pleased her as they needed a big catchup. The girls were quiet now. The monster stories must have worked because there hadn't been a peep out of them for an hour and the adults had settled down to a cosy evening in front of the wood burner. Ben thought the size of the television was a little too much, but he had to admit the film they watched looked great on it, and it was a detective movie, which he liked. Debs enjoyed the film too, but she now felt on edge because it was ten o'clock and Stewie hadn't returned. The snow that lay on the ground was now a couple of inches thick. She wasn't worried about Stewie driving in it, because he was a good driver, but she was angry at him because he had promised not to be late, so he could play Father Christmas, and fill up the girls' sacks. Still, Ben could do that, and he'd no doubt enjoy the experience, as long as he didn't wake the girls up!

Ben was enthusiastic about helping and he quickly filled their sacks to the brim. For some reason, the way he packed made them look like they were heaving. They successfully finished their secret mission and quietly tiptoed away from the girls room, fortunately they remained asleep!

'You made an excellent Santa,' whispered Debs, feeling grateful for the help. She felt so tired.

'Stewie's going to be late then, has he text you?' he replied.

'No, he hasn't, which isn't like him. That movie made me so sleepy, I could hardly keep my eyes open, or it could have been the brandy! I have to go to bed shortly or I won't be able to get up in the morning. I hope you're ok with that?'

'Yes of course, I noticed you were nodding, with the occasional loud snore. You used to snore and grind your teeth when you were a child,' replied Ben, then he laughed.

'I didn't,' said Debs who quickly realised her brother was joking. 'No, that wasn't me, it was you. Don't you remember the dentist explaining that you might have to wear something to stop you doing it, or you'd wear your teeth out!'

'I've still got my teeth though, haven't I? replied Ben with a toothy grin!

'Right,' I'm bolting the door and Stewie can sleep at his parents. It's half past ten now and he said he'd be back an hour ago. I've had enough of him never being around, he always misses the important stuff, and he couldn't even be here to help with the presents. I know it's mean but how and when, is he going to change.'

'You better let him know then,' Ben replied. He wanted to say that Debs was being unreasonable, but he knew better. She appeared a softie but when she'd made up her mind that was it, and even a snow-covered Stewie wasn't getting through that door tonight.'

'Yeah, I'll text him, but he won't be pleased. He has a key to his parents' house. He sometimes sleeps there, so it shouldn't be a problem. He's not coming back here at some crazy hour; he can come over tomorrow if he apologises.' Ben said good night and found his way to the spare bedroom. He was tired. Glasgow seemed a million miles away and he still couldn't believe that he'd driven all that way, but his body certainly did, because it was urging him to rest. He hoped that he wasn't going to be awoken by an angry Stewie in the middle of the night!

STEWIE AND GEORGIA – XMAS EVE

'Where are we going?' asked Georgia.

'Don't worry. I've driven this way dozens of times. It was too late to make that bus, and we'd never have got a taxi this late on Christmas Eve. I know it's about ten minutes longer, but it's the best way to go especially when,' answered Stewie, dropping his voice so Georgia couldn't hear the last few words, but she knew what he was saying, 'when I've been drinking.'

Georgia looked at her mobile. There was a text from her parents about their Christmas dinner tomorrow, asking what time she was arriving because they thought they would go out for a walk somewhere first. She thought it was a little late to reply, but it seemed rude to wait until the morning. She sent a quick message to say, sorry she was messaging late, but she'd been out with friends, and she'd be there at ten thirty. She loved spending Christmas with her parents, although they tended to stick with the same routine each year, a brisk walk somewhere in the countryside, then prepare the Christmas meal and later they would play scrabble or monopoly and watch the King's speech. Presents were usually early in the day, so she had a rethink and said she'd be around for nine thirty, which felt a little early after such a late night.

Stewie had the car radio on and was happily singing along to one of his favourite tunes, 'Midnight train to Georgia,' they often laughed about it. 'It reminds me of you,' he said, turning the sound up. Georgia closed her eyes and started to drift. The last thing Stewie heard was the last line of the song, then his Audi slid sideways, gathering speed as it rolled down a slope. When he opened his eyes, he wasn't sure how long he'd been out of it, because time had slowed down, and it was difficult to move. He couldn't see through the car windscreen because they appeared to be lodged in a huge snow drift, and the passenger side had been crushed in by a large oak tree.

'Georgia, Georgia,' he said, then discovered that speaking her name was almost impossible, because he couldn't hear himself. Where was he? Was he with Georgia, or Debs? He looked again and the memories of the evening began to unravel. He'd had too much to drink, but he hadn't planned on driving. He'd parked outside the office and was going to take a taxi home, until they went past the time of Georgia's bus. He then called his taxi company who refused to go on a huge diversion, and they couldn't get another taxi for several hours. He knew that Debs would go crazy if he arrived home far later than he said, so he decided his only option was to drive because he didn't want to leave Georgia in the lurch!

Despite Stewie's efforts, Georgia was unresponsive. Blood was trickling down the side of her head, which was resting on a huge branch from an incredibly gnarled oak tree, which now occupied the passenger side of the car. Stewie eventually managed to undo his seat belt to retrieve his mobile. He wanted to get Georgia out of the car, but his first aid training from many years ago, told him it was better not to move her and with trembling fingers he rang 999.

It wasn't long until the ambulance arrived followed by the Police. The paramedics carefully moved Georgia on a stretcher into the ambulance.

'We'll check you over, then you can go with her. But we need to do a breath test first to check you're not over the limit,' he heard a police officer say.

'Oh my God, over the limit. I just want to go with her.'

'Is she your girlfriend, or wife?' asked a very tall paramedic as they closed the doors to the ambulance.

'Neither she's a friend, a work colleague,'

'I think it's better that you come to the hospital later. She's in a serious condition and the Police want to talk to you about what's happened here.'

Stewie heard the siren as the ambulance sped off. Remarkably, he was uninjured, but in complete shock. 'It's Christmas Eve,' he mumbled. I'm meant to be Father Christmas. I need to fill up the children's sacks tonight.'

'Just get in the car Sir. You can explain all that down the station, plus there's a doctor who can check you over. You certainly don't sound right and it's way past midnight; you kept asking that. I'm sorry but you aren't going anywhere, it's too late for Santa Claus,' the burly Policeman stated bluntly.

Stewie then noticed a text message from Debs, which was sent at ten thirty, it said 'Stewie I'm fed up with being left in the lurch. You'll have to sleep at your parents tonight. Come over on Christmas Day when you've sobered up. I've bolted the door now and we've gone to bed. Happy Christmas!'

Stewie closed his eyes. After talking to the Police for some considerable time, he was taken to hospital to stay in overnight. The Police said that they would be back to talk to him in the morning. The hospital was reluctant to say anything about Georgia apart from her injuries were extremely serious, and they would know more soon. Stewie's life had gone from meeting up with an old friend for a quick drink, to a horrific nightmare. He also no longer had a car because the Audi was a scrambled piece of metal. His life seemed surreal, like being stuck in some bad movie, where he was playing the leading part! He felt sick and asked a nurse the way to the toilet and began vomiting through shock. He could smell the alcohol. Why had he been so, stupid when he didn't even feel the same way about Georgia! He was crazy to insist on meeting her right before Christmas. They had always had chemistry, a spark, connection, or whatever people called it now, but Georgia was a girl. In many ways she was naïve, that's what attracted him, her innocence and purity. Where Debs came across as the sensible, but boring, Debs, who thought it was more important to portray herself in a certain way to others, than to live her life for herself, although that had changed in the last few weeks. Stewie had a vague recollection of Ben coming to stay for Christmas, at least Debs wasn't alone. When she woke up in the morning, no doubt she'd be shocked to find out what happened because the police would be in touch with her, then there was the worry of Georgia's parents..

Stewie was relieved to find his way back to bed, at least he thought it was his because they all looked the same and it was very dark now. He would sort it all out in the morning, he thought, as his body gave in to much needed sleep. His last thought was he didn't want to face Debs, so he'd go to his parents. He knew they would be furious, especially John, but he couldn't go back to playing happy families. It was way too late for that, and besides how could he explain about Georgia. As darkness enveloped him, Stewie no longer saw light, only the horror of the old oak reaching inside his car to take Georgia, whispering 'You know you don't deserve her,' and for the first time in years, tears streamed down Stewie's face, as he revisited all his former disappointments, never having what he wanted because he wasn't good enough!

CHRISTMAS DAY

The following morning, Stewie opened his eyes, and the nightmare continued. He'd been told that he could leave after he'd been examined by the doctor, but he had to stay in contact with the Police, and he'd be given a date to attend Court because he was going to be charged. At least that would allow him the time to talk to his parents and Debs. If he couldn't spend Christmas with her, she still deserved to know what was going on!

The taxi arrived at his parents' house at eleven. After standing on their doorstep for ten minutes, Stewie realised that they weren't coming to answer the door, and his house key was with his car keys, which could be anywhere by now. Still in what used to be a car, or the Police had them. He managed to squeeze through a small gap at the side of the house, because they would locked the side gate, and get into the back garden. The swimming pool had its cover on now because it was winter and there was snow on the cover, which almost made it look like he could walk on it. For a few moments Stewie thought that as he no longer wanted to be here, that was an option. They would come back from their walk, or wherever they had been, and discover him face down in the swimming pool. Then he saw a vision of the girls opening their presents on Christmas Day, the ones that he'd worked so hard to buy, and pulled himself together.

The cabin looked cosy and inviting when Stewie opened the door, but as there was no heating, it was very cold. He found the gas heater that Sapphire used for her treatments in the winter and pressed the button to ignite it. Surprisingly, Stewie had never been inside the cabin because he wasn't that interested in his mother's work, although Debs had told him how cosy it was when she had reiki. As Sapphire could turn her hand to most things, he had no doubt that he'd find it comfortable. The therapy bed seemed a little high and it wasn't the best place to rest, but as he felt exhausted, he wrapped a blanket around him and with the assistance of the gas heater, he soon began to feel better. Were John and Sapphire visiting the children now, after all it was Christmas Day, so where else could they be, perhaps taking a short walk? They would be back soon as someone had to make the Christmas dinner, and it wouldn't be John!

Thirty minutes later, Sapphire put the nut roast in the oven. Surprisingly, she'd persuaded John not to have turkey this year, as there was just the two of them, and he'd be the only one eating it? As she stood up and glanced out of the window, she noticed a trail of footprints leading to the cabin. That's weird, she thought, hoping she hadn't left the door unlocked. Had someone stolen something, but what was there to steal, her couch, books, or candles? She quickly slipped her coat back on and hurried up the path. As she opened the door to her cabin, the heat hit her. It felt more like a sauna than a room used for therapy and to her surprise she noticed Stewie wrapped up in a blanket on her therapy bed.

'Mum, oh my God, did I fall asleep? I'm sorry, but I wasn't able to get in the house because I don't have my keys.'

'Stewie, we've just got back from seeing Debs and Ben. She called us this morning; after receiving a call from the Police saying you were involved in a car accident and being held in custody. I've managed to keep it from John, but he's not stupid, he knows something's happened.

'I wasn't in custody, Mum. I was taken to hospital in shock because I was involved in a car accident last night, the car slid and hit a tree. It's a complete right off.'

'So, you weren't over the limit?'

'Yes, I was over the limit. I was taking a work colleague home. We'd been out for a few drinks, and I was getting a taxi home, but then Georgia missed her bus. She lives in the opposite direction, and I had to drive her home, because she couldn't get a taxi, and mine wouldn't take her, plus it was snowing!'

'What were you doing going out on Christmas Eve, when you promised to help Debs get everything ready for the big day, and Ben was staying. Don't you think that's inconsiderate? What on earth's going on with you Stewart, you've been acting strange for months. It's like there's no-one at home. John tried to help by giving you money, but you don't communicate with us, and you're always on your mobile. Does Debs know about this other woman, and is she all right, or have you ruined her Christmas too? From what I understand she was taken to hospital in an ambulance.'

'I can't talk about this. I still feel sick,' replied Stewie who rapidly headed for the door of the cabin.

'Go in the house and lie down in the spare bedroom for a couple of hours. You can have Christmas dinner with us. It's nut roast and I need to take it out of the oven now and rescue the roast potatoes. I'll save you some to eat later. You do know that John's going to explode. He doesn't know all the details, but he will in time.'

'I have to go back to the Police Station later. They've discharged me, but it is a kind of conditional discharge, and I have to check in.'

'Great, so I now have to drive you there, on Christmas Day?' asked Sapphire in total disbelief.

'Mum, can't you stop thinking about yourself. It was an accident, and I know it's absolutely horrible, but what can I do about it now? I drove over the limit. I was bloody stupid. And now Georgia, who is a close friend, is unconscious in hospital. I don't know what else to say, I love Debs that's why I'm with her; Georgia is someone I met through the agency, whom I helped to find a job. We have been close yes, but there is nothing between us, just a Christmas catchup, that's all.'

'I hope you're right, Stewie, because not only will you lose your reputation and licence, which is awful, but being responsible for someone's life is an entirely different matter.'

Stewie walked through the snow back into the house and wished he was at the bottom of the swimming pool. Still, it was too late for that now, he would have to own up to what he did. This situation was escalating like a snowball rolling down a hill, gaining size and momentum in no time. What was he going to say to John, if he'd even speak to him because he often resorted to the silent treatment, which was far worse because no apology would bring him out of it.

John was preparing the table for their Christmas dinner, as he saw Stewie he mumbled, 'I thought you were coming over tomorrow?'

'Yes, we are, were. I'm not sure now Dad. Debs and the children are. I'm going upstairs to sleep because I had a really rough night, and I've got to go out later. I had an accident last night and hit a tree. The police said I was over the limit, I was! I'm now in all sorts of trouble, but I'm exhausted, so I'll talk to you later.'

John hastily walked from the dining room to the kitchen. Stewie was in trouble again; it followed him around. Why was he out on Christmas Eve in the snow, when Debs obviously needed him at home for the Christmas preparations and wasn't Ben staying?

He felt angry, but he knew there was little point in discussing it, when Stewie would have plenty of excuses as to why it wasn't his fault. Drinking though, it wasn't easy, especially at this time of year, but surely, he knew that the police were everywhere on Christmas Eve, so why hadn't he taken a bus or taxi if he had to go out? It must have been something important, or someone important to bother going out when it was snowing! Sapphire could have been right and there was someone else, although when she'd suggested that to him, he thought she was talking complete rubbish, stirring up more trouble in her imaginary cauldron. He'd switched off from Sapphire's notions since her transition from Susan. He loved Susan, why couldn't she return? He'd booked another session with the hypnotherapist in January because despite being annoyed that Simon knew his family and didn't say anything about it, he had to confess that he was drinking less. Drink driving wasn't a problem for him because he'd never do that, especially when working. However, Stewie was a different kettle of fish, he had this reckless way about him, where he dived into situations without considering the consequences. He hadn't got that from him. John thought it best not to talk about it. It was Christmas Day and discussing it would ruin the day for everyone; best Stewie slept it off. They would be able to talk about it tomorrow when Debs and the girls came over. He hoped they were still coming because he loved his granddaughters, and they would only visited them briefly this morning, to drop off the presents. Elsbeth was as bright as a button, she had a great future ahead of her. He'd already started to teach her a little chess, and she remembered all the moves and the little one's a diamond, always happy and laughing. It was shameful that their dad had ruined their Christmas over some selfish act! What could he say? One thing was for sure, if Stewie kept being destructive, he wasn't going to throw good money after bad, and he'd told him that on many occasions.

DEBS ON CHRISTMAS DAY

Debs didn't have to set her alarm this morning because at seven o' clock, the children were already opening their presents and screaming with excitement. She then heard Ben get up and go to the bathroom, they must have woken him, she thought, turning over in bed. She'd give them until eight, then she'd join them, but she then felt both Elsbeth and Florence land on her bed shouting 'Mummy, Mummy get up, look what Santa's left us.' Debs dragged herself out of bed and walked into the girls bedroom. Their bunk beds were covered in Christmas paper and presents. There were penguin shaped chocolates, stuffed toys, puzzles and games and they both had a pair of mini roller-skates, which were spread over their bedroom. Deb's heart sank when she thought of Stewie. She was happy that Ben was staying of course because she rarely saw him, but nothing was quite the same without Stewie who had been with her to buy the presents It was shortly after that when her mobile rang, and the Police informed her about the events of the previous evening. He must have asked them to call her in case she was worried, she thought, which she most certainly was, but until that point, she'd assumed that he was staying the night with his parents. He'd ruined everyone's Christmas and even though she felt sad about him not seeing the girls opening their gifts, she definitely didn't want to see him now! Her suspicions about him seeing another woman were correct, and even if Stewie apologised. she no longer wanted to know because his behaviour was unacceptable.

'Where's Daddy?' asked Elsbeth.

'Your Daddy's staying at Grandma and Grandads today, but we can see him tomorrow. What would you like to do now?' she asked, in an effort to distract them.

'Play monsters with Uncle Ben,' shouted Florence excitedly.'

Bunkle N got on all fours, growled, and started to chase the girls around the lounge.

'Ben, please try not to overexcite them,' pleaded Debs, it was first thing in the morning, and she wasn't ready for this, so she escaped to the kitchen. Her life was falling apart. Why had Stewie been such an idiot? How many chances had she given this man, but wasn't marriage meant to be through thick and thin? Her head ached, plus her heart was broken, and even worse she still felt sick, which had become a frequent thing over the past few days. As she put the roast in the oven and coated the potatoes with vegetable oil, she began to wonder when she last had a period. She simply had no idea, but it felt like a long time ago. She and Stewie never used contraception because they so rarely had sex, and he'd never been keen on condoms, but she didn't remember the last time he'd come near her, unless they had both been too drunk to remember! There had been another situation, which lingered at the back of her mind, but she pushed it away.

The next day was Boxing Day, and Debs couldn't face Stewie, or his family, so she decided, as the girls seemed happy at home with their presents and were enjoying Ben's company, to stay put. She felt awkward *due to her people pleasing habits*, but everything had changed since yesterday. The easiest thing to do was to send a text, but it would appear rude to do this on the day they were visiting, and it was Boxing Day!

Debs got up from bed feeling well rested. It was surprising how relaxing Christmas Day had been with her brother and the children, despite the awful news. She'd been able to sprawl out in bed, which enabled her to sleep well. She woke around eight, had a quick shower and went downstairs to make a cup of tea where she discovered Ben was already in the kitchen. He'd put the kettle on and was making the girls breakfast. What an absolute star, she thought he could stay!

'These children of yours are early birds, aren't they? I came down to make a cuppa, and there they were, declaring they were hungry. They're like a couple of little pigeons continually looking for food.'

'Yes, they are. It's so, good of you to look after them. They love their Bunkle Ben, I'm so glad you could stay. Would you like to stay all week because they don't go back to school and nursery for ages, it's such a long holiday.'

'Well, I can stay a bit longer Debs, but I'll have to do some work from here. I've got my laptop, so it isn't an issue. What's happening today?'

'I'm going to give Sapphire a call to let her know we're not coming. The girls are happy here, and with all this hanging over Stewie and his family, I don't think it would be a pleasant atmosphere for any of us.'

'Don't you want to see Stewie to talk things through. You know it will go to Court, and he'll get a sentence. It will be worse if the woman dies, it could be a seriously long time before you see him again.'

'I'm not saying that I won't see him, but not right now. I'm not ready for this. I can't face it. I know the girls will want to see their dad, but right now, I don't want anything to upset them. Plus, there is another issue she whispered, I think I might be pregnant. I keep rushing to the toilet to be sick and I don't want Stewie to know, not now, because it will only make things harder for both of us.'

'Pregnant, for God's sake Debs. How the hell did that happen?'

'I don't know Ben, I'm as shocked as you are? One thing is for sure, it's best not to tell anyone because I'm undecided what to do about it.'

'I see. Would you like me to take the girls to the park, feed the ducks or something? It's freezing out there, but I'm sure the ducks would appreciate some bread. It will give you some space to call Sapphire. What a strange name, did she pick that herself? Don't you start Ben, John's always going on about it. Her real name is Susan, which he prefers because when Sapphire became *her authentic self*, John didn't appreciate it, and he wants the old version of her back! They have their own issues to deal with, let alone Stewie's!'

After the girls had finished their cereal and marmite toasted fingers, Debs and Ben set about dressing them up for the extremely cold weather, plus finding some stale bread from the bread bin for the ducks. They were excited to go out with their uncle, and it was only a ten-minute walk to the park.

'See you soon,' shouted Debs, knowing that in this temperature they wouldn't be gone for long!

Sapphire answered her mobile phone. She was prepared for Debs backing out because she'd be in shock, and things would be challenging with Stewie.

'Okay, I understand, but I'm disappointed at not seeing you and the girls.'

'How's Stewie?' Debs asked, quickly changing the subject.

'Things don't look good. Georgia's in a coma and the doctors don't have any idea if she'll pull through.'

'Georgia,' answered Debs.

'Georgia, his work colleague. If you want to come for Reiki in the New Year, let me know and we can have a chat about it then, it might help us both to talk things through.

'Perhaps, but I'll probably keep going to see Simon, we're making good progress in our sessions, and he's still helping me with childhood issues.'

'Ok then, you know where I am if you want to talk. I have to go now,' Sapphire replied, briskly.

Debs could tell she was upset but was it because she refused the offer of reiki, or because she was spending time with Simon, or both! One thing was for sure, right now she needed space from them and the easiest way to do that was to stay at home.

APRIL

It was Sunday, and a beautiful spring morning, at the beginning of April, and Debs looked out at the children in the garden. Wow, they've grown. They were playing with a large coloured ball, making a load of noise to let off steam. She was pleased that she'd cut the grass yesterday, as it looked lovely and it was easier for them to play without getting damp shoes. It had been over three months since she saw Stewie. She'd had a few phone calls from Sapphire, because they wanted to talk to the girls on the telephone, but that was it, and as the children were still so, young, there wasn't a lot of conversation. Debs explained to Sapphire that when things were settled, she'd be in touch, so she and John could see the girls. Despite being on her own, she was managing fairly well. Working part time helped, as it enabled her to get some of the domestic jobs done while the girls were at nursery and school. Debs finished putting a big pile of clothes in the washing machine, she'd wash up the breakfast things and keep an eye on Elsbeth and Florence, through the kitchen window. They wouldn't go far and thankfuly they didn't have a pond or swimming pool to worry about. Their house was a relatively small three bedroomed semi, but the garden was a decent size, and it looked great when the grass was cut. At least it didn't need a great deal of maintenance.

The doorbell rang unexpectedly. Who on earth could that be at nine thirty in the morning, Debs thought? She quickly hurried to the door; she didn't want to take her eyes off the girls, but if there was a problem, no doubt she'd hear them. She opened the door slowly and was surprised to see Sapphire standing on the doorstep. She was wearing blue jeans, and a stripy loose-fitting jumper with black leather ankle boots.

'Hi Debs, I'm sorry to call this early on a Saturday, but I'd like to talk to you. I miss the girls so, much, I just wanted to pop in and see them, is that all right? I know how difficult things are, but Stewie has his Court date, and it made me think that he could get a sentence, and be away from us for quite some months, although his Lawyer seems to think that he'll only get six months, considering the circumstances, first offender and all that.'

'What about the girl, Georgia. Is that her name?'

'She's out, thank God. I've been telephoning the hospital regularly. They wouldn't let us see her, not even Stewie, but at least we know she's out of hospital now, and back living with her parents. It's all so awful. It's torn our lives apart. Now I don't see you, nor the girls, and things are difficult between John and Stewie, they don't even speak. Stewie seems depressed. He knows he did the wrong thing and how awful it's been for everyone, but it would really help if you'd talk to him Debs.'

'Come in for a few minutes, Sapphire. We can't talk on the doorstep because the neighbours will hear us. Would you like a cup of tea? I'm ironing, but I can keep an eye on the girls out of the kitchen window, they're in the garden.'

'Tea, yes, that sounds good, and perhaps I could say hello to the girls?' asked Sapphire shakily.

'No doubt they'll come haring in as soon as they see you.' explained Debs, as she went to put the kettle on.

'Excuse me for saying so Debs, but you look flushed. Are you unwell?'

'I'm fine. I wasn't going to tell you this, Sapphire, but it will be difficult to hide soon. I'm well, but I'm pregnant.' Sapphire took a sip of her tea and sat down on a chair out of view of the window. Debs thought she looked shocked, and before you say anything else Sapphire, Stewie isn't the father.' Sapphire looked puzzled, as she wondered how on earth anything else was possible!

'I may as well tell you the truth, although I don't think you'll be happy. Simon is the father, and it was totally unexpected.'

'Simon,' muttered Sapphire who suddenly appeared pale.

'Yes, Simon, like I said. It wasn't planned, but we've started a relationship. That's one of the reasons why I haven't contacted Stewie. I didn't think this would help him, when he needs to focus on getting the best outcome in Court.'

'He certainly does,' replied Sapphire, whose whole demeanour had changed.

'The girls are happy about it. I told them a couple of days ago. I went for my first scan last week, and Simon came with me.'

'I can't believe you've done this to us. You've been totally selfish. Don't you know what we've been going through, and you just move on, and start having a relationship with someone else. You know how I feel about Simon, no wonder you've kept it to yourself! I won't say hello to the girls today; they haven't seen me yet, and I'm not in the mood to play happy families now. I think I'll be off. You know Simon's not meant for you, don't you? He may appear loving and charming, but you don't know him as well as I do. Wait until the baby comes. He likes his independence, and he has a very selfish streak. I can't imagine him being a father.'

'It isn't your choice though, Sapphire, and forgive me for saying this, but you sound jealous.'

'What me, jealous. Debs, you have so, much to learn. If you'd paid a bit more attention to Stewie, then he wouldn't have strayed in the first place.'

Debs felt an unwanted anger rising inside her, which wasn't good for the baby, nor herself. If Sapphire had only known how indifferent Stewie was towards her, wrapped up in his work, his financial problems, and never being at home. When was she supposed to pay him more attention.

'Weren't you leaving?' Debs asked, walking towards the front door.

'Yes, I am, and don't worry, your secret's safe with me because I wouldn't want to upset Stewart any more than he is. He's got enough to deal with. I'll contact you about seeing the girls in a couple of weeks, after the Court Case.'

Debs declined to answer and quickly opened the door for Sapphire to leave. She heard her speed off in her sports car. Sapphire was never short of money.

The girls ran in from the garden asking for drinks and biscuits. They would been outside for an hour and although it was sunny, there was still a slight nip in the air. 'Go in the lounge and I'll bring you some drinks. 'Why don't you watch that film, and I can finish the ironing. Where's the tv controller?' she asked them.' she asked them.

When Debs returned to the kitchen and went to pick up the iron, she noticed she hadn't stood it up, and it had burnt a huge hole in her favourite blouse, which was stuck all over the iron. 'Shit,' she shouted, but fortunately the girls hadn't heard as they had fully emerged themselves in 'Frozen.' 'I hate ironing, and this stupid blouse doesn't fit me anymore,' she muttered, as she chucked it in the kitchen bin. I guess it's time for loose fitting clothes, or possibly maternity wear!

THREE YEARS LATER AND JESSICA

Jessica adored her Daddy. She followed him around like a baby lamb looking for direction, and Simon was a brilliant father. Debs felt happy. Taking a step back from Stewie's family had been a good idea. Simon didn't have much of a family being an only child. His parents lived in Cornwall. They had planned to visit them this year because they had never met Jessica, and she was already three. The girls adored her sister, apart from when they tried to pull her red curls, everything was fine. Jessica's hair was such a deep shade of red, Simon referred to it as auburn. She was a little darling, and very well behaved most of the time, at least Debs thought so. Life was going well with their three little girls. Sapphire visited them once a fortnight, but always on her own, and she often took the older two to the park, saying that she couldn't really cope with Jessica. It gave Debs and Simon the chance to have one-to-one time with their daughter, either doing a little puzzle, or playing with her in the garden, watching her on her tiny swing or slide, which she loved.

Simon's work schedule was full, and Debs had been offered another day teaching, which she planned to do when Jessica went to nursery. Her life was full enough and she didn't want to overstretch herself, but they did have to pay for a childminder for Jessica on the days she taught at the school. Sapphire was arriving at twelve o'clock today and then staying for lunch, which hadn't happened before, but as Sapphire had said she wanted to talk to them, Debs thought it a good idea. Since Sapphire appeared to have accepted her and Simon's relationship, things had become a lot better between them.

Debs and Sapphire sat down at the kitchen table to eat lunch with the girls, which was quite simple and consisted of cheese on toast with crisps followed by yoghurts. Florence and Jessica had children's yoghurts, and as Jessica was so little, she had to be helped. After lunch, the girls went to play with their toys, and said they would look after Jessica, allowing Debs and Sapphire to have a short time to talk.

'Stewie has been training to be a counsellor; would you believe it? After he'd been back home a few months, he realised that he needed a complete career change. Things had never really worked out that well for him in the employment business. After the accident, he realised he needed a lot of therapy himself. Honestly, Debs, he's like a different person now. I'm happy to have him living at home with me. It was a tragedy at the time, but he's moved on. The girl he was friends with, you know, the one in the accident, Georgia, got married last week. He found her a job you know. He had a phone call from someone who worked at the same company as her, I've forgotten what they're called, but she'd been dating someone from work for quite some time, and they are really happy. This man contacted Stewie about recruitment not realising that he'd closed everything down, he obviously doesn't read the newspapers! I'm happy the girl met someone, especially after what she'd been through. Stewie said he's a good bloke; I don't think they'll be inviting him to the wedding though!'

'No, probably not,' replied Debs, who didn't want to continue with their present line of conversation.

'We'll have to have the girls for the afternoon soon. It's just Stewie and I at home now because John moved out a few months ago, he's living near Edinburgh. He wanted to be in Scotland to play golf. He's working in some country practice, which suits him down to the ground. It's big-time golf country there, and he wants to retire early. He says there are so many great courses, he's in his element. He'll come to stay from time to time, so he can see the grandchildren. We are still friends, but it's difficult for me. It broke my heart when he left, but there was no way forward for us. We are two quite different people, at least it frees me off to do what I want. I know that sounds selfish, but I felt controlled by him. Even though I had the cabin, and I was free to do my reiki sessions, I felt judged and humiliated. It's interesting that since he's left, I have more clients. They don't say, but they may have sensed our energy wasn't right. I'm at the end of my yoga training now and I want to do something with it, I don't know if I told you about that?'

'Yes, I think you did,' replied Debs, who felt subdued. 'I need to check on Jessica. The other two will be all right, but she's still small,' she said in an effort to escape and get some air.

'Isn't she like Simon? She's got that bright-eyed intelligent look, just like her father. I'm not sure who she gets those red curls from, but she's definitely got his spark. Anyway, I mustn't hold you up any longer, thanks for the lunch, and for letting me see the girls. I have a client later, so I need to get things set up.'

Debs saw Sapphire to the door then gave her a quick hug and peck on the cheek and closed the front door. She didn't have to say much to get under her skin these days, but at least she was trying. Debs felt some compassion for her because it must have been tough with John leaving. What a shock for her, but she was right, they couldn't carry on as they were, it must have been miserable. Stewie sounded like he'd changed too, but she still didn't feel like communicating with him. If the girls went over to their house, she guessed she'd eventually have too. At least that girl, Georgia, had found someone. Was she simply someone Stewie had helped to land a job? She might never know, but whether he was involved with Georgia or not, their own relationship hadn't been right, and it would have taken an awful lot of energy to change it, certainly more energy than she wanted to invest! She walked into the lounge to find Elsbeth and Florence sitting together on the sofa watching cartoons, and Jessica had fallen to sleep holding her cuddle blanket on her favourite chair. She smiled at them; she loved them so much. Her children were her life. She enjoyed being a mother, especially since Simon had come into her life to support her. He'd gone out for a bike ride today, but he'd be back soon. He liked to keep fit whenever he had the chance. They had planned a walk in the woods tomorrow and were taking a picnic. Life was busy, but it was good.

STEWIE'S NEW START

Stewie sat by the side of the pool. Living with Sapphire was working well for him, at least for now, because he didn't have to worry about bills. It was a roasting hot July day, and his feet were dangling in the water to cool off. Sapphire was busy giving a client reiki in the cabin. He didn't know how she did it because it was red hot first thing, but with the door open and a couple of fans blowing, no doubt it would cool down fairly quickly! Hopefully, it would feel different by three, when he had his client for counselling, which was a lady that Sapphire recommended, a reiki client. He was pleased that he'd been able to make a start. He had three clients last week, and their initial sessions went extremely well. It gave him the confidence to believe that he could build a decent business over time. As Sapphire was fairly busy, she'd agreed that he could use the cabin when she was quiet. She always started early morning and finished around three, which worked well for both of them. He was grateful his mother had been so supportive over the last few years because clearly his father didn't want to know. Communicating with John wasn't worth the effort, when he was unlikely to visit often, only once in a while to see the grandchildren. From what he understood from Sapphire, he'd started a completely new life and loved his job at the country practice. He guessed he still had time to play golf!

Stewie was much changed, according to his mother, but he also felt the change within himself. He was still troubled by occasional nightmares in which he dreamt that the huge oak came to life and took Georgia away, but more recently he dreamt it was Debs who disappeared. His mind was still confused at times, in a similar way to straight after the accident, when he didn't know what on earth had happened. He realised that he'd sabotaged his relationship with Debs, by practically ignoring her when she needed him the most. He'd grown bored of her constantly complaining she was tired, and hadn't supported her, vanishing to the office at all hours and having little consideration for her feelings. He found it hard to admit that he hadn't realised how much she had been struggling. Georgia had been a distraction, an attractive younger woman, someone he could focus on to make him feel good about himself. He'd wanted a bit of flattery. He'd also wanted sex. After talking to his counsellor, he realised his part in this, and how badly he must have hurt both Debs and Georgia. *The root cause of it all was based around his rejection and abandonment issues,* but hadn't he abandoned his own family? He really missed Debs and the girls. Debs had dropped them off for a couple of hours recently, so he could see them and play in the pool, but they hadn't spoken to each other, apart from a quick hi, or goodbye. Her excuse was always that she couldn't stop because Jessica was in the car, and it was hot. She didn't want to stay for more than a few minutes, and she never took Jessica out of the car, which wasn't that hard to do!

Jessica, according to his mother was a beautiful and intelligent child, with long auburn locks. She was bright as a button and had a fascination for a doctor's kit, which she'd found in the girls' room. Neither Elsbeth, nor Florence appeared the least bit interested in it, but Jessica had listened to the heart of all her teddies and sneaked up on the girls to listen to theirs too!

Stewie laughed out loud, when he thought about it, then remembered that Sapphire was still with her client. It was ironic that the child who was interested in being a doctor wasn't even his! Could this Simon guy have been like that as a child, interested in the medical world? Who knows, Sapphire obviously liked him because she was always mentioning him. She had found it difficult to accept Debs and Simon were together, which was understandable, but he didn't want to discuss it when he had his own feelings about their relationship.

It was now two forty-five, so Stewie slipped on his trainers and smartened himself up in preparation for his client. He still felt tremendous guilt about Georgia. He'd thought about writing to her many times since the accident, especially during the time he was in jail, but somehow it didn't feel appropriate. What would he say to her, sorry would never be enough. When he heard about her wedding, he decided to send a card. He'd thought long and hard about what to write in it, but as he knew them both, having had close connections with the company they both worked for, he decided to just go for it. He picked out a card, which said, 'Good Luck on Your Special Day.' It was blank inside, which was fine as he wanted to keep things simple. He then wrote 'To Georgia and Justin all the best for the future, Stewie,' with a single kiss. He sent it to the office rather than Georgia's room because it was doubtful that she was still there after all this time. She may well have moved in with Justin or have a new house together. He smiled; thank God that chapter of his life was over. He missed Debs so much. What an idiot he'd been. He wondered if he called at the house, she'd speak to him. He'd discussed it with Sapphire who had warned him to leave it, saying she was now living with Simon, and they had a child What was the point when they were never going to get back together? He had to learn to accept things as they were. He had to learn to accept things the way they were. He knew that he needed to focus on his new career, but he couldn't help his feelings. He walked into the house hearing the doorbell. His mother's client had left five minutes ago, and no doubt she'd be hurriedly tidying the cabin, *clearing the energy for the next person with some of that sage*. Stewie had learned to love the cabin and the aromas that permeated from there. It was always uplifting, and he now had a different attitude about reiki since he'd seen his mother's clients positively glowing at the end of their sessions.

'Hello Julie, wow, we've got a warm one today. We've had all the fans on in the cabin, so we won't melt, and there's a jug of water. Would you like to come this way, take a seat.'

Stewie's sessions normally lasted ninety minutes after which, he was definitely going for a swim in the pool. It would help to clear his head, then he could decide if he had the courage to approach Debs. The *meditation* that Sapphire had been teaching him over the last few months had also been a life saver, and he was understanding more about *staying in a positive space.*

'Is there anything that you'd like me to focus on?' he asked, Julie.

Julie a plump, middle-aged woman, who was already going grey, was wearing a short flowery summer dress with a scooped neck. She crossed her legs nervously and started twiddling her fingers.

'My father, she said, tentatively. 'He wanted me to become a head teacher. I was happy teaching, but I had no desire to be head. All that hassle and responsibility, it wasn't for me. He was a bully, he's not around now. He died a few years ago from a heart attack, but he never let up all my working life. I haven't worked for over a year, due to stress and anxiety. It seems ridiculous because he's dead, but I can still hear his voice talking to me and feel his expectation. As far as he was concerned, I'd never made the grade, and it made me feel *like I wasn't good enough.'*

Stewie went silent for a few moments. He tried *not to be triggered* by this, because he knew that he'd meet many clients who had similar childhood circumstances to his own. He suddenly remembered his breathing, which had recently become a redeeming quality. 'We'll work on that,' he replied, 'we can write him a letter.'

Stewie felt empowered and aligned helping others. Why hadn't he trained in counselling, or even coaching years ago, yet he already knew the answer to that. Julie unexpectedly smiled at him then said, 'I can see how it would help to get it all out on paper. Where shall I begin?'

'The very first time he said something that didn't feel right to you,' answered Stewie empathically. We'll talk it through and then I'll give you a little homework!'

'That's easy. It was when dad took me away from all my friends and put me in a private school, which I absolutely hated. He insisted that this school was better at teaching academic subjects, when what I wanted to do was to learn drama!' replied Julie with tears in her eyes.

'Yes, let's start there,' replied Stewie.

LIVING IN SCOTLAND

In the very charming courtyard garden of the Sheep Heid Inn, Duddingston, on the outskirts of Edinburgh, John was drinking a cool beer and waiting patiently. The sun was out, and a gentle breeze rippled the leaves of the surrounding trees and plants, creating an ambient atmosphere. He felt happy. Living in Duddingston had been a massive change, but a positive one. He'd started his new life in Scotland by renting an apartment in Edinburgh, but as he worked at a surgery in Duddingston, it made more sense to rent a house near his work, in the village itself. Today, he was out on his first date with a lady who worked at the surgery with him. They got on really well at work, having instantly clicked, which surprised him because in many ways she was quite different. Susan was a trained acupuncturist, and of Chinese origin and he found her incredibly attractive. The way she expressed herself was unique, being gentle, kind, and courteous. She also appeared interested in what he had to say, their connection being a blend of mutual respect and friendliness. Susan had also mentioned an interest in bird watching, so today, after their meal, they planned to visit Duddingston Loch to watch the herons and great-crested grebes.

John leaned back slightly in his chair and stretched. He felt a little tired, but nowhere near the fatigue he felt while living with Sapphire, which had zapped him, particularly when she talked about Stewie. He planned to visit her and the grandchildren soon, but for now it would have to wait, as he had golf matches, and a new woman to focus on, or did he? He found it hard to imagine why Susan had accepted his invitation to lunch. She was younger, ten years or so, possibly mid-forties, and incredibly attractive plus they shared similar interests, which was a good place to start.

John looked up from his phone and suddenly noticed Susan walking from the pub to the garden where she stood in front of him. She looked stunning in a pale pink blouse, with smart blue jeans, and she smiled at him.'

'Hello Susan, do come and sit down. I picked up a couple of menus, and I expect they'll be around for our order soon. I must say, they seem pretty busy here, I doubt we'd have got a table if I hadn't booked. The food must be good, have you visited before?'

'Yes, a few times actually when my brother visits. He lives in London, he's a doctor.'

'Oh really, I expect we'd all get on rather well then.'

'Yes, we probably would.'

They stopped chatting, while Susan scanned the menu to search for something vegetarian, then discovered there were one or two new options since her last visit.'

'Oh, your vegetarian,' remarked John.

'Yes, I've been vegetarian for years, my health is much better as a result.'

'Like my wife,' replied John, wishing he hadn't.

'Are you married? You didn't mention that. What's her name?'

'Her name's Sapphire, but she used to be called Susan. It's a long story; she's a reiki therapist. We just grew apart. It was no-ones fault, it just happened. We became two quite different people, who could no longer communicate.'

'Susan, really, so I guess I'm Susan two! Did you have a problem with her giving reiki treatments?'

'No, not at all, it was good for her actually. It wasn't the reiki, there were many reasons why we grew apart, somehow, we couldn't bridge the gap.'

'We can't escape from what we are here to learn John, but we can discover something valuable from the experience,' replied Susan, taking a mouthful of vegetarian lasagne.'

'That's interesting, I'm sure it will dawn on me in time what I'm meant to learn, but right now I'm happy to be where I am. I love Scotland and the new job's working well.'

'I love it here too. I like the simplicity of things, that's why I enjoy bird watching. There's always something new to discover. When you look closely at nature you realise that it's only humans who flap because birds take things in their stride.'

John laughed, then cut into his pork. It didn't matter if Susan two was a vegetarian like Susan one because nothing was going to change his taste for meat. 'I'll tell you more about it when we walk around the Loch,' said John and you can tell me why you're not wearing a wedding ring. I assume you're single?'

'I'm single. I've never met anyone that I clicked with, although I do believe that opposites attract. You can learn so much from each other.'

The sun suddenly became strong on that part of the garden, and when their plates had been cleared, they decided not to worry about dessert or coffee. 'Let's get a coffee later, after the walk,' John suggested.

'Yes, but I'll have a green tea,' replied Susan smiling.

This lady will be a bit of an education for me, but am I willing to learn, pondered John. Susan's pale pink blouse set off her dark skin, and jet-black hair in a way that he would only describe as radiant beauty, So surely, he could make a few compromises, if he only knew where to start. He hoped this afternoon's bird watching would give him some pointers.

John and Susan really enjoyed walking around the lake. They both had binoculars and the conversation between them was easy and relaxed. John had his notebook and wrote down anything unusual he saw, while Susan appeared to get quite excited by their findings. It dawned on John that becoming involved with someone from work might not be such a good idea, especially if they fell out, then things could become awkward. He wanted to keep this connection in the friends zone for as long as he could and build up trust between them. He wasn't sure what Susan wanted, and as she'd just discovered he was married, it may have put her off any thought of romance. They could simply enjoy some 'bird watching walks together,' and see how it goes. One thing was for sure; Susan was immaculately turned out. Her expensive fashionable clothes set off her trim little figure, and he couldn't help but feel a strong attraction for her. Thankfully, she hadn't arrived in the hippy shapeless trousers that Sapphire wore because that would have been a complete turn off!

Susan suddenly pulled him from his thoughts, 'have you seen the heron on the far side of the water, it's looking for fish.'

'I see it. This Loch is brimming with wildlife, what an amazing place,' replied John enthusiastically, and what a fabulous afternoon. We must come here again.'

'Definitely, it's so close to both of us. You lived in Bristol before, didn't you? Isn't there a great bird reserve near there?' Have you been?

'Yes, Slimbridge, it was only about thirty minutes away because I lived in Frenchay, which was on that side of the city. I worked as a consultant at the hospital for quite a few years, but I much prefer doing what I do now because it was manic at times.

I went on my own; Sapphire was never interested. After a few years, I put away the binoculars and they gathered dust.'

'Well, there's plenty to see around here. My former husband wasn't interested either. I left him about six years ago, fortunately, we never had children, or it would have made things a lot more difficult.'

'It most certainly would. I have a son and grandchildren too, two gorgeous little girls. I hope to visit them soon. They also have a new baby sister, well she's not so new now, a few years younger than the other two.'

'It all sounds pretty busy and your son, do you see him?'

'Not unless I can help it,' replied John, drawing in his breath. 'It's a long story and a difficult one, so I think we'll save it for another time. Shall we find a place to go for coffee now?'

'Yes, I think we deserve it, don't you?'

John smiled at Susan two and started up his BMW. It was amazing how quickly his life had changed over the last few months. He genuinely hoped Sapphire was happy. She sounded as if she was, and Stewie had started his new counselling career, to which he was far more suited. Well, good for him he thought. No doubt they would pass a few words when he visited, but whatever Stewie did from now on, he'd never be that interested, because his son had crossed one line too many and he didn't intend rescuing him!

SIMON

Simon took his racing bike from the small shed, at the rear of Bellevue Mansions. He'd left a hasty note for Debs to tell her that he was going for a long cycle ride, so he may not be back for a couple of hours because it was a beautiful day.

Debs awoke to the sound of Jessica screaming, she was fighting with her sisters, but then she remembered Simon was off work today, so she would be able to have a long soak in the bath. She was aware he was up, but assumed he was just making a cuppa, or catching up with his appointments on his laptop. When she saw the scribbled note on the kitchen worktop, she felt a little annoyed because he'd never said anything about going out for a cycle ride the previous day, and they would previously planned to go out as a family, to the garden centre. Well, I guess my long soak in the bath will have to wait, she muttered as she started to make the girls some toast. Finally, she sat down with a cup of tea on a comfy chair in the living room. The children seemed content to munch through their breakfast with their plates on their laps, while watching a cartoon. It was a bad habit,

Debs knew they would be better at the table, but she wanted them to be happy.

Her phone buzzed and to her surprise she noticed it was a text from Stewie. Debs decided to open it because they hadn't spoken for so long, apart from making short arrangements about the girls and was secretly curious as to why he'd contact her.

'Hi Debs, can I pop over and see you soon? There are some things that I'd like to talk over privately, not in front of Mum. Let me know when you can spare half an hour. I'd be happy to come to yours to make it easier,' Stewie.

Debs thought it was likely about the girls, so she replied, 'ok, will do,' to keep it casual.

When Simon arrived home a few hours later, he was sweating. It was already a hot day, and going out on his bike ride had obviously been quite a workout.

'I'm dripping,' he said wiping his forehead with his sleeve. 'I'll take a shower, then I need to talk to you about something. I haven't forgotten about the garden centre, but we'll wait until after lunch now, shall we?'

Before Debs had the chance to reply, Simon disappeared. She put the kettle back on for a second cup of tea. The girls seemed calm and happy. They would have a look for some plants for the front borders, then take them to a big park, so they could have a run around and a picnic tea. It was the summer holidays, so there wasn't a rush to get back, or they could even get fish and chips. They loved going there.

Simon reappeared; his hair was still wet, but he looked like he was glowing. He was wearing some denim shorts and a white polo shirt and appeared more relaxed.

'Debs, a friend of mine is setting up a retreat in France and needs a hand with the yurts and gazebos because it starts the following week. I've offered to do short hypnotherapy sessions, past life stuff, and there's yoga, pilates, a nutritionist, plus other workshops, juicing, that sort of thing. If I go it would be for a month. Do you think you can manage on your own for the next few weeks?' Simon asked.

For a few moments Debs was dumb struck. Four weeks, this wasn't how she visualised her summer. What could she say, she didn't want to put a chain on him, then again, it appeared a little selfish, and what about Jessica, didn't he want to spend time with her over the summer? Before she could say anything, Simon replied, 'I knew you wouldn't be pleased, but it's only for a few weeks and you know how I like my freedom.'

'It's up to you, but I can't pretend to be happy about it. I thought we were going to meet your parents and have a holiday at the same time,' she replied, suddenly feeling a little shaky.

'When's Stewie coming over? Can't you go out a few times as a family with him while I'm away? I really don't mind if you want to do that, Debs.'

'No, I don't want to do that, that's why I left him because I'd rather spend my time with you.'

'Well, he's still your husband, you're not divorced yet, and he has the right to see the girls. I was trying to be considerate.'

'When's Stewie coming over? Can't you go out a few times as a family with him while I'm away? I really don't mind if you want to do that, Debs.'

'Things will always be complicated because the three of us have been together in many lifetimes. Do you remember that meditation where I saw a Native American life, Stewie and I were brothers. He lost you in that life too because he was abusive. Eventually, he was forced to leave our tribe because the elders wouldn't tolerate him. It was difficult because I was his brother. I looked after you and the baby. It's a repeating pattern and we have to resolve it.'

'Resolve what, Simon? It's resolved because I'm with you. I don't care about past lives rubbish. I know it appeared real in the meditation, but do you really believe Stewie was your brother? I don't mean to belittle your work, but I don't believe in *past life regression*, that's why I've never asked you to do it! I think your *hypnotherapy treatments* are amazing, so I don't feel the need. I've got to get the girls ready to go out now, Are we still going out today? Stewie's coming around to talk to me about the girls, but that's all it is. There isn't going to be any big reconciliation. I thought you wanted to be with me?'

'I do want to be with you Debs; I'm only going away for a month. I've always been a free spirit and although we have Jessica together, when we go out there's always three of them, and to be honest, I sometimes find it hard work. I'd welcome Stewie seeing his daughters a little more, but right now, I feel like I need a bit of a break. Whether you agree with past life regression or not, it's what I do and I can't wait to join the retreat in France. It starts in a few days, so I said I'd go.'

'Fine. I'll take the girls out on my own and you can stay and pack. I may as well get used to it,' Debs said as she frantically looked for the car keys. 'Girls come on, we're going out to the park, the big one next to the garden centre.' Debs' heart was pounding; she wasn't sure if it was fear or anger, but she didn't like it. Sapphire's words came into her head about Simon liking his independence too much to be properly committed, which made her feel worse.'

Simon looked out of the bedroom window and watched Debs drive away. *He knew she'd react like that because she was insecure.* He loved her, but he didn't want to be owned by anyone, that's why his previous relationships fell apart. *Co-dependency was a horrible feeling, two individuals losing their sense of identity and in doing so, they lost the very thing that had drawn them together in the first place.* Debs needed more independence, he'd be happy to look after all three children if she wanted to go on a retreat, or holiday with a friend, but she didn't appear to want to do anything. He could see why it hadn't worked with Stewie. There was always the other side to a story, him having an affair was all wrong though.

Simon quickly found a suitcase under the bed, which contained his passport in one of the back pockets. Fortunately, it was still in date and before he knew it, he'd packed shorts, T-shirt s and trousers and had begun to get the taste for traveling. 'Sod it,' he said out loud as he dialled the number of a local taxi firm. 'Yes, to the airport please,' he found himself saying. He'd already looked at the flight times the previous day and discovered he could fly with Easy Jet straight to Bordeaux and there was a seat on a flight later this afternoon. This was madness, Debs will be livid, he thought as he booked the seat, but the way he felt right now, nothing was going to stop him.

The taxi arrived thirty minutes later as Debs arrived with the children at the park. Debs was pushing Jessica on a swing, whilst watching Elsbeth and Florence on a roundabout, when her phone buzzed.

'Hi, I managed to get an early flight, see you in four weeks, love Simon x.'

Debs looked at the text in total disbelief, selfish pig,' she thought. Sapphire was right, Simon had a side to him that she knew nothing about!

STEWIE TWO WEEKS LATER

It was a bright day in early August and Stewie parked his car at the front of 7 Bellevue Mansions. He enjoyed living with Sapphire, but seeing his home again made his heart ache to be back, although it looked slightly dowdy since he last visited. Obviously, this Simon bloke wasn't into DIY because the paint on the front door and windows had started to peel, and it could do with a new lick of paint. Stewie smiled to himself because he couldn't remember the last time he picked up a paintbrush; surely it wasn't that long ago!

Debs appeared at the door. She looked very serene in a short-sleeved cotton patterned summer dress and, for the first time in years, Stewie thought she looked confident and attractive.

'Hi, come in, we can sit in the garden. The girls are out there having a picnic, and it's not even lunch time. They put it together themselves and who could blame them in this glorious weather,' she said.

'Yes, it's hot, so I decided to put my old denim shorts on. I expect you remember them; they're getting a little holey now, but I can't see myself throwing them away for a while!' replied Stewie with equal enthusiasm. 'You look cool in that summer dress, is it new? Wow haven't the girls grown. I know you came over a few weeks ago, but they are changing so quickly, and their baby sister isn't a baby anymore. Did she get those red curls from you? I don't remember seeing curls in your baby pictures.'

'No, I don't think so, they're from Simon's side of the family. I bought the dress from the charity shop down the road, so it's kind of new.'

'I've missed you Debs. Oh yes, I almost forgot I have a present for the girls. You can hang it in their room; it helps to keep bad dreams away!'

'Wow, that's amazing,' she replied pulling the brightly coloured dream catcher from its paper bag. Brown and gold feathers, that's lovely. You won't believe this, but Simon has one just like it hanging over his therapy couch, with the same colour feathers.'

'What, here in the house?'

No, in his therapy room. In the flat where he lived when I met him. He still sees his clients there.'

'Oh, spooky!'

'So, you have two men in your life who like the same things.'

'Simon thinks you were brothers in a Native American life, and you had a fight over me, which led to you being kicked out of the tribe.'

'Like being kicked out of my house?'

'I didn't kick you out Stewie. You can visit whenever you wish.'

'He sounds a bit of a nutter, believing in things like that, just like Sapphire. She loves all that past life stuff. She keeps telling me who she was in different lives, and I tolerate it, but most of it's her imagination. I'm grateful she's sharing her cabin though, especially as it's so precious. My counselling sessions are going really well, and I've been able to fit in more clients since she's been away.'

'I'm so happy for you Stewie, that's great, but I didn't know Sapphire was away, she didn't say anything.'

'A yoga retreat in France, or something. They were short of someone for their yoga workshops, so she's gone over there to help. It hasn't been long since she finished her training, but she's keen to get going with the teaching. I think she's back in a couple of weeks. She couldn't have picked better weather for it, although I'm not sure it's the same in France. I saw thunderstorms on the weather, and it's extremely humid there.'

Debs was dumbstruck. It felt more than a coincidence. Simon would say it was synchronicity-that he and Sapphire happened to be away on a retreat at the same time! Would Simon stay faithful to her? What would happen if Sapphire made a move on him? In her fifties, she was still an extremely attractive woman, and Debs thought that she'd never completely got over him leaving the group!

'She must be at the same retreat as Simon, he left about two weeks ago and he'll be gone for another two. He left early to help put up gazebos and yurts. He's giving short hypnotherapy sessions.'

'The gazebos were up weeks ago, Sapphire showed me some photos of them before she left. It looked great, very restful. I might give it a look next year because I'm sure I'd enjoy some of it. I hope I haven't upset you by telling you about Sapphire. We don't even know if it's the same retreat. It's near Bordeaux or something.'

'Yes, that's the one,' replied Debs, feeling annoyed that her mother in law's whereabouts had been kept from her.

'I don't know why you're upset Debs, nothing's going to happen between them. I know Sapphire fancies him, but honestly, I'm certain she still loves John because she talks about him all the time. I doubt she'd admit it though, besides Simon isn't interested in her. He's living with you, and you have a child together.'

'And we, have two children together,' replied Debs, who suddenly felt that she was connecting with the real Stewie. The one she knew before they lost each other.'

'I know,' he replied touching her hand, which she pulled away from because the children were demanding more blackcurrant squash and crisps!

Debs quickly got up and walked into the kitchen leaving Stewie with the girls. Sapphire was right, Stewie had changed, he had started to listen. She shouted from the kitchen would he like a cup of tea and then put the kettle on. For some unknown reason, Stewie appeared more interesting, but her heart ache was about Simon, or was it? Wasn't she plain fed up with him doing whatever he wanted? Did he want to be with her or was she merely a convenience. At the most crucial time of the year, when she had the girls on her own for weeks, he disappeared on her. Was it really that difficult for someone to stick around and support her, or did she drive men away?

'Here you are, have a builder's tea, I didn't think you'd want herbal.'

'Actually, I'm partial to a mint tea in the cabin,' he said with a grin, but I save the Earl Grey for Sapphire.'

'Flip me, you have changed,' said Debs as she gently touched his hand back. What was going on with her? She'd never flirted in her life, and now she was flirting with her husband!

'It was my fault, Debs. I didn't realise how hard it was for you, looking after the girls and working. It was tough for me too, but I should have talked to you. We stopped communicating, and the sad thing was, we still loved each other. At least I loved you and still do.'

'Don't Stewie. It's way too late. I have another child now and I made the choice to be with Simon. I know it may have been a rash decision, but at the time it felt like the right one.'

'And how does it feel now?'

'Well right now, I'm angry with him because he disappeared on me. We had a bit of a row over him going on this retreat, so I took the girls to the park on my own and while I was there, I received a text to say that he'd already left.'

'What a cunt,' muttered Stewie, forgetting Debs didn't like swearing.

'I was furious, but what could I do? If I appear insecure about his freedom, it will only push him further away. He's a good dad to Jessica, but I don't know if he's cut out for family life. He said that it's tiring taking the three of them out. I think he'd welcome you spending more time with Elsbeth and Florence, or them staying overnight with Sapphire. You know that I had my reasons for not wanting that to happen too quickly, after what we went through. I was so devastated by the whole thing that I found it hard to forgive you.'

'Can you forgive me now? It took me having counselling to see your perspective. I never loved Georgia. I was looking for a way out of the mess I'd created. She was never you Debs. Our short relationship and it was short, wasn't what I had with you. I can see it all clearly now. I'd really like us to be friends, especially as Simon doesn't appear to have a problem with my visits, and he'd welcome me around the girls more. Let's take the girls out together. It's great weather and it would be a shame to waste the opportunity. I'll check my appointments and send you a text. Decide where you want to go and I'll drive us. How about the beach? It's a long time since we went to Weston Super Mare?'

Debs smiled, that was a long time ago, before she had the children and fitted into tiny bikinis. They were good times, and she was much slimmer now, so who knows, she thought, feeling a positive glow.

'Ok, I'll have a think.' The girls were already excited at hearing 'the beach,' and came running.

'No, no, not today,' Debs said firmly. We can go next week if your dad's free because he must check his schedule.

'We have two dads, don't we Mummy?' asked Florence.

'No, you have one daddy and Simon,' replied Debs, and Jessica has Simon.

'Where's Daddy?' Jessica asked.

'Daddy's gone to France with Grandma,' replied Debs, who still felt disgruntled.

THE RETREAT

It was a glorious August day, and Sapphire had just finished teaching her yoga class. Surprisingly, it was packed full. There had been twenty-five of them and they had to move outside on the grass because there wasn't room for everyone in the gazebo. The class was a real mixture of males and females of different abilities. Sapphire was in her element. She'd started with the basics so everyone could join in, then she brought in a few more advanced exercises for those who could manage it and kept the others with easy stretches. As there weren't many advanced pupils, she was able to put them into one group, and it worked well. She suddenly noticed Simon at the back of the room. Sapphire wasn't completely surprised to see him, as she knew he was friends with Lara and would have known about the retreat, but she didn't think that he'd come in the middle of the school holidays! It wasn't until she'd had a proper look at the list of workshops that she saw his name, under past life regression. It appeared that the previous man they would booked who was French, was unwell and had dropped out at the last minute, so Lara must have asked Simon to cover at short notice.

The class rolled up their mats and stacked them in the corner of the gazebo for tomorrow's class, which was at the same time, eight. It felt right for the group to exercise before breakfast and have the rest of the day free. Simon waited until the participants dispersed, then walked over to Sapphire holding a large bottle of water.

'Hi Saph, I saw you were running the yoga retreat, so I decided to join in. Lara asked me if I could help when Andre dropped out, but it was a bit last minute. My leaving in a hurry really upset Debs and we've hardly spoken since, but I've known Lara for years. It was difficult for her to set up everything on her own.'

'Yeah, I can imagine Debs is upset, because it isn't the best time to leave her with three kids in the middle of summer. But I get it, these opportunities don't come along that often and I know you love your freedom, the same as me.'

'I thought you'd understand Sapphire, with us being so alike. I know she's your daughter-in-law, but she's not always the easiest person to get on with, is she, there's a lot of expectation and control.'

'I wouldn't call Debs controlling, perhaps a little inflexible at times. I think Stewie's been in touch with her whilst we've been away, so they'll be able to take the children out together. It would be nice if they were friends, better for the girls.'

'I don't have a problem with that; I'd welcome more input from him. Anyway, if you want to try *past life regression*, I've got some slots free this afternoon, but I'm already filling up. As we know each other, I'll give you first refusal.'

'I can't come this afternoon, Simon, but I can make it late tomorrow afternoon. There's so much to see here and there's a folk band I want to see a bit later, that I've liked for years. Can you fit me in around four tomorrow?'

Simon looked at his mobile then said, 'actually, that works well for me, Saph, I'll see you then. If I can move a few people around tomorrow, I'll come to your class. It was great. I haven't done yoga for years; I was stiffer than I thought.'

'If I can do it at my age Simon, you certainly can,' Sapphire replied, followed by a smile.

'Yes, see you soon. I'm joining the meditation in Gazebo 11, now,' he replied.

Simon walked away taking large swigs of water. It was so hot and humid that he also poured a little over his head, wiping his forehead with his sleeve. The retreat was brilliant; he was having great fun. It was a pity that Debs had gone stone cold on him, was she *ghosting him*? He'd text to say that he arrived safely, but she hadn't bothered to reply. He looked at his watch and hurried to join the *meditation*. They could have a long chat when he got home. Things had to change For their relationship to survive, it had to be free and flexible and that's what he wanted.

Sapphire felt a little jaded but continued to smile. She'd only just finished her training and had been plunged into teaching a class of twenty-five, how did that happen? She thought about joining the meditation but didn't want to appear as if she was following Simon. Her attraction for him was stronger than ever. He was such a *free spirit*; it was impossible to envisage him married and settled down. Despite Debs numerous therapy sessions, she was still going through *bouts of insecurity*, which pushed men away. It was odd, but her intuition told her that Stewie was the best match for her, despite what he'd been through because he genuinely loved her. It was written on his face. If it hadn't been for Jessica, she wondered if Simon would be there. He must have been shocked at becoming a father so quickly, when he'd always given everyone the impression that he wanted to stay single. He wanted to travel and have new experiences; there was no way that this man was settling down type. Tomorrow would be interesting because she and Simon had shared so many lifetimes together, that when he realised how closely they had been connected, he wouldn't be able to deny their attraction.

Sapphire drank a huge glass of water, then ate an energy bar, hoping it would lift her before looking for Lara to say hello. At the front of her was a jacuzzi with a group of six young men and women. She thought about going to get her costume to join them, then noticed they were lying on the grass naked in the sun. At fifty-five, Sapphire had an incredible slender body with shapely legs, but she didn't want to be naked, so she stripped down to her underwear and laid on a rug on the grass.

'Hello, I'm White Bear,' said a voice next to her. I was in your yoga class, this morning.'

'White Bear, that's an interesting name. I'm sorry I didn't notice you, but the class was very full,' she replied.

'Full, they'll be even more tomorrow. You did a great job. I really enjoyed it. Where are you from?'

'Bristol,' she replied, as she closed her eyes, being unable to resist the strength of the sun.'

'Interesting,' I'm from Bath, we're neighbours. I offered to be a first aider here because I'm a doctor, or I was a doctor because I'm now into alternative medicine.'

'Big Bear,' she mumbled.

'No, White Bear,' he replied, 'that was my name in my former life.'

'I'll remember that now,' she said, then smiled.'

'Do you want to go somewhere to have a chat? There are some relaxation gazebos, with cushions to chill on, we're getting cooked here,'

'Yes, why not, it would be good to hear about your life as a doctor and what led you to such a drastic change. It must be quite a story.'

'It most certainly is,' he replied, as he stood up and started walking to Gazebo 9, which was the most comfortable looking space Sapphire had seen for a long time, apart from her cabin of course!

'What sort of tea would you like, they do a good chai here, shall I order two?'

'Yes please. I'm parched after all that yoga talk, having to raise my voice so people at the back could hear,' explained Sapphire.

'You sounded nice and clear. If you like, I can take the beginners tomorrow and we can split into two groups. I've taught yoga for years.'

'Really, fantastic. What caused a doctor to retire so early?'

'It was during COVID. We both had it, but my wife was very sick. Marge eventually recovered, then had all the jabs and who knows what happened next. It was easy to blame on covid because she'd had it a few weeks before, but they called it an unexplained death. It was tragic. It happened in 2020, and I'm still not over it.'

'It's hard to know what caused it under those circumstances. All I can say is that the unexplained deaths have increased, and people accept it as completely natural. It's certainly a difficult thing to evaluate, best to be open-minded.'

'It's not natural to die in your mid-fifties when you are over the virus. After that, I examined all the science and concluded that a lot of it was unsubstantiated. I was forced to move on because I could no longer work as a doctor once I'd delved into conspiracy land. That wasn't the best plan either because those tunnels don't appear to have an end. While all this was going on, I decided to have some hypnotherapy, as I became a compulsive smoker and the therapist suggested past life regression. At the beginning I laughed at the idea, but then I decided why not, if it helps. The life I had as White Bear was interesting. I was a leader, and I didn't follow the pack in that life either. I found the whole experience liberating. It's not something that I choose to talk about unless I'm at these types of events, or around people who think like me.'

'Wow, fascinating. I can't wait to have mine. I've seen many of my lives as flashing images during meditation, but I've never been able to pinpoint any of them. I think it will help me too. John and I *broke up because of my beliefs,* him being more *in the logic,* and me being *a creative.* I'd have loved it if we had found *some sort of balance,* but he *ridiculed me.* I was goldilocks with her coven. If I complained about it, he became worse. Our old friends would laugh, and *I felt humiliated,* but I didn't want to spend time with those people anyway. *As soon as I began reiki my friendships changed. People that I'd known for years fell away, and others stepped in.* At first, I was unwilling to let go of friendships that no longer served me, but as time went on and *I worked on myself,* I learned there is more than your biological family. *My soul family* were appearing out of nowhere and these people didn't need to know all my history because they accept me for who I am. Much of our happiness is built on acceptance. I guess it could be argued that your wife was *still suffering from Covid,* as *some people had long covid.* What a tragic story, I'm so sorry.'

'I'm getting through it now. Yes, we're all seeking acceptance, I completely agree with that. I was adopted. There's always been a part of me that never felt fully accepted, but that's another story. Would you like another cup of tea?'

'What I'd like to do is sleep,' Sapphire replied, as she laid back on a bed of comfortable cushions.

'I'm going to leave you to dream. I think people have been smoking in here, and it's knocked you out. Rest, and we'll see each other at yoga tomorrow, if not, before. I'm going to check out the sound healing, I feel very drawn to that,' he said.

Sapphire lifted her arm to wave goodbye, but found sleep came more quickly than it ever had before! Surprisingly, she dreamt about John, she was visiting him in prison. His *soul wanted to be free*, but he remained *trapped by his own judgements*. They wouldn't allow her to see him, and her heart was breaking. She stood on her tiptoes to look through the bars and standing there was White Bear, not John! What was going on? How could John be White Bear? She had wanted John to come back for so long, and now for some reason, her heart asked, '*What do I miss about him, he's never going to change.* As Sapphire opened her eyes, she was surprised to find tears on her face. She felt that she had something to learn this weekend, and it was beginning to emerge. The gongs and windchimes which echoed through the trees began to draw her in. They sounded like the beginning of a new song, a sound that she'd never experienced, which was resonating through her body, with familiarity and comfort. Sapphire stood up, put on her sandals, and walked in the direction of the sound not knowing what she'd find, but with a feeling of excitement building within.

*   *   *   *   *

The next day Sapphire found her yoga class a breeze, with the help of a very enthusiastic White Bear, whose real name was Tom Jones! No wonder he preferred people to call him White Bear, she thought with a smile on her face because his name was a lot to live up to. Tom came from Wales and had an extremely charming Welsh accent; he'd moved to the Bath area after attending Bath University many years ago. He'd lived there ever since. There were far better prospects in Bath than where his family lived in Wales.

Tom was enormously helpful with the beginners, which gave Sapphire plenty of time to concentrate on the more complex yoga moves. When her class was over, she thanked him, and they decided to return to Gazebo number 9, for a further chat before Sapphire headed off to her hypnotherapy session with Simon. She was now starting to feel a little apprehensive. What if she didn't like what they discovered? It was possible that she'd done something terrible in a past life and might find it difficult to accept. Tom said that she was worrying over nothing, and she shouldn't be so intense about it. He was more interested in her relationship with

John, wanting to know where he'd studied, and about his practice in Edinburgh.

'White Bear's a great name, but I'd prefer to call you Tom, if you don't mind. If you can't get over the Bear bit. I could call you Tom Bear? I understand why you wouldn't want to be called Tom Jones. I expect you've been ridiculed about that most of your life but surely, there are many men called Tom Jones in Wales?'

'Yes, there most certainly are. It was mainly ignored when I lived in Wales because we were as common as mud, but for some reason when I was at University, I was teased quite a lot about it, with, give us a song Tom, and sometimes I would oblige to get people off my back, but singing has never been my thing. Contrary to belief, not all Welsh men are good at singing.

'*Coincidentally, (although that doesn't exist)*, I also changed my name. I was quite straightforward Susan, who in a way represented very normal Susan, perhaps because we were the second most popular name in 1959, and it's been popular ever since.

'So, you *felt ridiculed* by your husband, you say, *you didn't see it as an affectionate form of teasing.*'

'No, I didn't, it was degrading. He made me appear like some mad woman who'd totally lost the plot. He was happy for me to do what I wanted, but *I was unable to talk about it or share any of my beliefs* with our circle of friends, some of whom would have been happy to hear about my reiki, but by the time he'd stamped 'coven' on it, I didn't want to go into long explanations about the *benefits of meditation and spiritual development. I was censored!'*

'Oh yes, I can understand that. I had *a huge awakening moment* shortly after my wife died, when I changed my beliefs about many few things that I was previously adamant about!'

'John was a big follower of the science, most doctors are. Many of us therapists and I know quite a few, are still labelled as obscure and a little eccentric. It really depends on what type of therapy you do because some of them which are practiced in surgeries, appear to be more respectable. Ironically, John is now dating a work colleague in Edinburgh who *practices acupuncture*, and she's called Susan. No doubt that's what attracted him in the first place. He hated me becoming Sapphire. Sapphire with the red hair and baggy clothes, how unattractive!'

'I don't know about that, wasn't there a song called 'baggy trousers,' which was quite a hit!' replied Tom.

'Tom Bear, now that's the sort of teasing, I'm comfortable with!' replied Sapphire, giving him a playful nudge.

Tom was a tall man with a good head of dark hair. Sapphire assumed he was the same age as herself and she smiled at his big and slightly out of control beard. He was also chunky. The sort of man who gave great *hugs like a bear*. He'd obviously been devasted by the *death of his wife* and was still working through that, but there was something very comforting about Tom Bear. He was a good listener and didn't dominate conversations, not like John. Mind you, if John didn't want to hear something he just cut off and pretended he was deaf. Once again, she became very sleepy sitting in Gazebo 9 and suggested they walked around together for another couple of hours until Simon was ready at four.

SIMON AND SAPPHIRES' PAST LIFE REGRESSION

Sapphire wandered into Simon's healing Tipi and was immediately greeted by a strong smell of incense, with Simon dressed up in full Native American Indian wear, which totally surprised her. He had various wooden instruments around him. One of them looked like a huge rattle and another an unusual looking drum.

'Hi Simon, I'm not really feeling this today,' Sapphire said, as she looked at him. His hair, which had grown long, was drawn back into a ponytail and he wore an exotic looking shirt and headband.

'Well, that's up to you, Sapphire. I've done six today already, so if you're not feeling it, perhaps we ought to try another day.'

'Will I be safe?' she asked suddenly.

'Of course you will, you'll know what's happening all the time and if you appear distressed in any way, I'll quickly bring you back.'

'I know this sounds silly, but what if I don't like my past life and it interferes with the happiness I have now.'

'That's the point though, isn't it, to release and become happy. People are regressed because they need to heal something in their current life, and one of their past lives may be impacting it. Are you really happy now, or just relatively happy?'

'I'm happy, but I do miss John, and I never thought I would.'

'What do you miss about him?'

'I miss our family gatherings because our Sunday roasts were really special. I miss Debs, Stewie and the children coming over, and eating together as one big family or going for a walk.'

'But you told me that John ignored you, and straight after the meal, he'd go off and do his own thing. You also said on many occasion that he was a control freak, and that's why you spent so long in your cabin avoiding him. You also didn't enjoy his company, remember when he asked you to go bird watching, you didn't want to compromise on that, because it meant spending more time with him. I know you said this to me, a long time ago, when you apologised for asking me to leave the group, but you were adamant about it. Do you think that you're missing family life, rather than him? After all, you still have Stewie living with you. You and Stewie could eat meals together.'

'Yes, we do, but I liked that getting together thing, but you're right, when I think about the way John behaved, he did ignore me. He also drove me mad saying Stewie would have been better working as a doctor. I don't remember telling you about the birdwatching though, maybe he told you that?'

'It doesn't matter who told me. What you need to think is, do I want to listen to that again? Or if not that, some other rant, or form of control. I can't influence you Sapphire, but as we're friends, I can remind you how you felt. It's so easy to forget.'

'And what about you and Debs, are you planning on going back to her?'

'Of course, I am. I'm allowed to take breaks away; Debs is still my partner.'

'I know what you think, Sapphire, that I'm not capable of family life, but time will tell. Debs knows that I'm *a free spirit*, so, it's really up to her. Anyway, shall we get started, then we can be in time for the communal food at six.'

'I think as you told me I'll be safe, I will be. Let's go ahead.'

Sapphire lay on a comfortable bed covered with a selection of patterned blankets and looked up at the roof of the tipi while Simon counted. It wasn't long before she drifted off into a beautiful, relaxed state. The energy of the tipi changed, and she very soon became aware of the sound of a crackling fire. She was seven years old, and her hair was long and straight, and what people would describe as black. She clutched a bow and arrow and went to play in the field next to the tipis, which was full of butterflies. After she'd been playing for a while, she heard a voice calling her, it was her father who was the chief of the tribe. His face was heavily painted in different colours ready for tonight's ceremony, to celebrate their harvest, and to give thanks and gratitude. Two children appeared near to her. One was a boy the same age as her. He was her friend and a twin. Sapphire suddenly felt afraid. What are you afraid of Sapphire?' asked Simon, as he became aware of her distress.

'I don't like the second boy. He's mean and he won't leave me alone. He wants to play games like jump over the fire. I don't want to do this, but he says if I don't do as he says, he will hurt me. The other boy, his twin, tells him to leave me alone and to let me do what I want. I see them squabbling and I'm running away because I'm afraid.'

'Does anyone seem familiar to you?'

'Yes, the chief, my father, he feels like you. He doesn't look like you, but he is still you, and my mother, yes, I can see her too, that's Debs. None of this is real. It feels like I'm stuck in an old movie, what's happening to me?'

'Just breathe and relax Sapphire. This past life we share can hold great insights for both of us. Yes, I'm with Debs, she's by wife. Stewie left the tribe a few years ago, and then they made me chief. You are our child.'

'Who are the other children? Who is the mean and controlling one? It gives him power, and he forces me to do horrible things.'

You know who these are Sapphire, but it isn't the right time for me to say. You will know and when you do, you'll be able to release things and move on.'

Sapphire became aware that she was dressing for the ceremony. She felt a sense of excitement as there would be dancing and entertainment. The drums started to beat, and she sat on an old wooden stool, which had been carved out of a tree stump. A beautiful blue butterfly landed on her hand to say hello, and she began to hear the sound of Simon's voice saying that he's bringing her back.

'Sapphire, Sapphire, are you alright, come back now and be with me in the room.'

Sapphire opened her eyes.

'Simon, oh my goodness, that was incredible.'

'I'm glad you're back. For a minute there I thought you didn't want to return. I was beginning to panic!'

'What, you said I'd be alright!'

'Well ninety nine percent of people are, but there's always one or two that are so comfortable in that dimension, they don't want to return.'

'You were my father in that life?'

'Yes, I was, and I was meant to take care of you, but I let you marry the wrong twin and after that things didn't turn out well for you. He grew up to be a nasty bully and I didn't realise it.'

'So why didn't you leave me in this past life to find out what happened? Who were these two boys, the bully and the nice one who took care of me?'

'Yes, the other twin did care for you, and he wanted to be with you, but he was pushed out.'

My guides tell me that you already know who the controlling one is, but the other twin is called White Bear, you may get to meet him sometime. I have no idea how that would happen, or when, but you'll feel you know him, when you do.'

'White Bear,' whispered Sapphire in complete disbelief, but surely there are hundreds of White Bears! She smiled, then turned to Simon and said, 'that was incredible, life changing.'

'I'm supposed to look out for you in this life because I didn't take care of you in that one. There's also a lot of past life issues between Stewie and I, that we're still working through in this life. That's why I couldn't say about my future with Debs, because it's not that straight forward. If Debs can forgive Stewie, then it's the end of our *soul contract*. I only vowed to look after her, until Stewie evolved enough to take on the responsibility that he'd shirked in the past.'

'It sounds like a story, Simon. It's hard to believe it's real.'

'It's as real, or unreal, as you want it to be Sapphire.'

Sapphire got down from the couch and drank some water.

'I need to chill for half an hour and have a cup of that great chai tea, then I'll see you at dinner. I feel very ungrounded right now, very floaty. I'll take a walk in bare feet. I've got a friend waiting for me.'

Sapphire gave Simon a hug and kissed him gently on the cheek.

'See you later,' she said turning on her heels and smiling. She knew White Bear was waiting for her in Gazebo 9, so she headed in that direction. As she began to walk, her mobile buzzed and surprisingly there was a text from the man who never text! She opened it tentatively.

'I thought I'd come down next weekend to see the grandkids, if you're back from your shenanigans in France! I miss you, Goldilocks. When I'm home, let's have a proper chat about everything. John xx'

Sapphire looked at the text in utter astonishment. It wasn't what she expected to see. So, John planned on coming next weekend, but she felt no sense of excitement. Her need for John had completely disappeared the minute she realised the torturous abusive boy in her regression was him. *There were many forms of torture, it didn't have to be physical.* She'd tolerate him for the sake of the grandchildren, but if he was having regrets because he'd been dumped by Susan, she didn't want him back! Simon was right, *she had been addicted to control, confusing control with what she'd thought was an interesting challenge.*

'Hey, how did it go?' asked Tom Bear.

'I need to go back and look at control,' she replied looking serious.

'Wise idea, fortunately no-one can control a bear,' he replied, then smiled.

'It was fascinating, not at all scary and it explained so much. My ex just text and asked if he could come and stay next weekend to visit the grandkids, if I was home by then?'

'What did you say?'

'I'm going to say yes, but he'll have to sleep in the spare bedroom.'

'Being free from control is the road to abundance because love is unconditional. If there's control, it isn't love,' Tom Bear explained, lightening the situation.

'Tom Bear.'

'Yes,' he replied.

'Are you ready for dinner?'

DINNER WITH SUSHAN

John had a sense of excitement that he hadn't experienced in years. The last time he felt this way was the lady in red moment he had with Susan, when she dressed up in a red silk dress, and they would smooched together for hours. 'Smooched,' he laughed. Did people even say that now? Danced intimately, or maybe close together? He'd thought about a tie, but concluded it was way too formal, so he wore his best black jeans with a deep red shirt and smart grey jacket. He'd always liked red; it represented energy and passion. Sapphire said it was *'base chakra,'* why on earth was he thinking about that now, when he was going to meet Susan. There was no doubt in his mind that she would look gorgeous, classy, and elegant. They were driving into Edinburgh, and he was picking her up in about fifteen minutes. She lived in the same village, which made things simple. Their whole relationship had been easy, having started off as work colleagues and more recently, they would become close friends. He had never once crossed that line into the romantic zone, as Susan had made it clear that for now, she didn't want that. Perhaps tonight would be different, as they were having a romantic meal, where the *energy*, another Sapphire word, could easily change.

John sprayed his favourite aftershave, Creed's Green Irish Tweed, gelled his hair and looked for his leather jacket. He looked good and was pleased with his appearance; all the walking he'd done over the last few weeks had definitely paid off.

John got out of his BMW and knocked on the door of Susan's terrace cottage, which was brightly painted with window boxes full of geraniums. The cottage had the same sunny disposition as its owner!

'Hello,' wow, you're early, my nails are still drying,' said Susan, as she stepped outside.

Susan looked incredibly beautiful. Her perfect skin and beautiful long dark hair, rested on a pale blue dress, which came just above the knee, with the addition of a fashionable dark denim jacket. John looked at Susan's elegant slim fingers with indigo nail varnish, and simply said, 'I'd better get the car door for you, then.'

Once they were inside the car, John explained he was going to surprise her. They were going into Edinburgh Old Town, which was only a short drive. Susan smiled, she was happy to spend time with John because he was fun to be around and always appeared positive. She'd agreed to go to dinner, but he needed to be kept in the friend zone, as it had become increasingly obvious to her that he wasn't over Sapphire. When he returned home, there was still a chance that their relationship could rekindle, and Susan didn't want to be the woman caught in the middle of anyone's marriage.

They parked in a car park and walked for five minutes until they reached The Doctors, a place John had visited several times, whilst living in Edinburgh, he loved it. It was historic and had links to Edinburgh University and the old Royal Infirmary. John thought it had real character. 'Where would you like to sit?' he asked politely.

'Oh, I don't know, anywhere comfortable, but not right in the middle, or everyone will knock into us. It's already busy.'

'How about here, Susan,' he said speaking above the noise around them, as he pointed to a comfortable window seat with a large conservatory to the rear.'

'By the way, John, my name isn't Susan, it's Sushan. It's like Susan but pronounced differently. I know it sounds the same, but it's not.'

'Oh really, when I've heard your name spoken at the surgery, it sounded the same to me.'

'That's because you're English, it's the Chinese version of the name. Look it up on google if you don't believe me.'

'Oh, I believe you, subtle differences can soon add up to big ones,' replied John, clearing his throat. He was starting to feel awkward.

'Shall we order now before it gets too busy, or we'll have a long wait? I don't see much for vegetarians on the menu, but I suppose I could have fish!' said Sushan, who didn't want to dwell on differences!

'Great, I'll get us a couple of scampi and chips. I had that last time. It was excellent.'

'I'm not in that much of a hurry, I might take a little longer. Ok, just go and order now because it's packed.'

John stood up, walked to the bar, then shortly arrived back. 'Just as well we ordered quickly because it looks like a coach load's arrived,' he said with a smile, suddenly touching her knee.

For a few moments Sushan looked shocked, then decided to speak up. She'd experienced several relationships where she hadn't been able to express her feelings from the start and had vowed that if anyone tried to move too quickly again, she'd speak up, rather than wait until things became difficult to change.

'John, you know we're good friends and I like that. Your great fun and we've had some interesting walks, particularly as we both like bird watching and wildlife. You're also a great colleague, but I don't want to be your girlfriend. I've recently been thinking that I don't want to be anyone's girlfriend, I'm happy as I am. I'm not your lady in red, your Susan. I'm quite different. I know you miss the old Susan, but I'm not her, and I can never be her.'

John's face suddenly looked red. For a few moments he appeared angry. He'd never imagined for one moment that Sushan was his lady in red, but now as Sushan said this, the pain in his heart was immense. He'd obviously told her more than he intended and who was he trying to kid. This young lady was years younger than him, and she'd never promised him anything other than friendship, yet she looked so attractive tonight that he couldn't help but push things a little further by caressing her knee. He instantly removed his hand as soon as he felt her tense, because it was obvious to him at that point that she didn't want this kind of intimacy, and now Sushan appeared to be picking at her scampi like a sparrow. She obviously wasn't keen on the meal after all; then again, he hadn't given her much time to read the menu. *Was this what he was like? He thought that if he took control, and led her slightly, she would like it, and respond in a positive way, but what was happening was the complete opposite.*

'I never thought you were her,' John replied, as he munched through his chips, taking large mouthfuls of scampi. As soon as they finished the meal, they were going to leave. There wasn't going to be a dessert. All the images he'd had of them strolling hand in hand and kissing her perfectly shaped lips, whilst stroking her beautiful dark hair, had come to a grinding halt. He felt humiliated. How dare this woman treat him like this. Referring to his marriage in such a way was degrading. Sushan knew nothing about his relationship with Sapphire, only the snippets that he'd told her on their walks, and she certainly wouldn't be able to understand the depth of his feelings. Sapphire was his *soul mate*, she was irreplaceable. All she needed to do was to stop dying her hair and wear some decent clothes, which he'd buy for her, so she didn't have to look like that! He obviously hadn't shown her enough love. He looked over at Sushan, who had decided to tuck into the chips. It was obviously the scampi she had a problem with. He'd visit Sapphire next weekend, when she was back from that hippy camp in France and tell her how much he missed her and hold her tight. He wanted to hold on to someone or something because he was going crazy. He loved his job, the area he now lived in, and playing golf, but he'd never felt so empty in his life. God this was awful. He had to admit to himself for the first time that some of this was his fault. *Was he a control freak, and if so, how could he change*? He thought he could meet Sushan halfway, but this was never going to turn into a relationship and that's what he wanted a relationship, not this best friends rubbish. How could a hot-blooded man, who fancied an attractive woman, be expected to be just friends, when all he wanted to do was touch her. He was pleased that he'd text Sapphire before he came out for dinner. He missed her despite his sexual attraction to Sushan. It was definitely time for them to talk. Sapphire hadn't replied yet, so maybe she was still in France. What if she'd met someone? It had been a long time since they had communicated, so there was a strong chance she had met someone new, being an attractive woman. Not as attractive as Sushan, but still a bit of a looker, when she wore the right clothes!

'I'm happy for us to be friends, but let's make one thing clear, you're not like Sapphire. You are more sociable, fun to be around and we have things in common. I think it would be an idea to skip the dessert though, as I really don't rate them here. They are pretty overpriced, and I was going to suggest sharing one, but that's a little intimate under the circumstances!'

'The Chinese always share food. I possess a 'lazy susan' for rotating food, so everyone can reach. It's put in the middle of the table. I'll have to cook you a meal someday so you can see.'

'Yes, that would be great,' John replied, as he tried to wipe the smirk off his face. It seemed an *uncanny coincidence* that the name should come up again, and one thing was for sure; this woman certainly wasn't lazy, she was one of the hardest workers he knew. It still made him smile. He looked over at Sushan and she was smiling too. That's spelt the way you know it, the English way,' she said. They both laughed. John felt the ice had broken, so they decided to stay for coffee before making their way to the car.

'I really enjoyed the meal, but I'm trying to pass on desserts, as I'm piling on the pounds,' said John.

'I've heard it said that sugar's more addictive than cocaine,' replied Sushan.

'Right now, I could do with the latter,' thought John who didn't feel the need to reply. As he put his phone in the side pocket of the car, he noticed that Sapphire had sent a voice message. He was dying to listen to it but decided to wait until he was home with a whisky in his hand, and a dose of rubbish tv, which unfortunately he hadn't managed to give up!

John dropped off Sushan giving her a quick peck on the cheek before she left the car. Then five minutes later he walked up his path and unlocked his front door. The new sofa he'd bought was extremely comfortable, so he slumped back and opened up the voice message from Sapphire.

'Hi John, I'll be home by next weekend. I've had a wonderful time at this retreat in France, but I'll be happy to return home, camping gets a bit tough after a week or so! The girls will be pleased to see their Grandad, and Stewie will be pleased to see you too; he's getting on great with his therapy clients. Just send me a text when you are on your way, so I've an idea of when you're arriving and can be home, although I expect you still have a key. I'll make up the bed in the spare room.'

John felt a pain in his chest. He missed his grandchildren, and he missed Bristol, although this was something he'd only experienced in recent months. His life in Scotland was absolutely great, but there was nothing like having family around. Life was unpredictable and he didn't expect the reaction he'd received tonight from Susan. He'd always call her that, even if it was pronounced differently. What do women want? it was a mystery! Perhaps because he'd been out of the dating game for so long, he'd become blind to women's needs. He had a stable career; his finances were in order, and he now worked out at the gym, plus played golf on his days off. He considered himself to be in fairly good shape for a fifty-six-year-old, and although he certainly wasn't Pierce Brosnan, he had a certain look about him, which had been described in the past as attractive. He poured himself a whisky. After trying dozens of these new channels on the television, he found nothing grabbed his interest. He turned to the book he was reading. He was an avid reader of crime, but this book was psychology. He wanted to understand himself better and why he felt the need for control. Deep down, he had a lot of regret about going out on a limb and moving to Scotland. It worked well for golf and his career, but he was starting to feel there was more to life than this. Was it family life, support, *spiritual fulfilment* or just having friends? Susan had been the only woman he'd met since moving here and that was because they worked together. He didn't want to go down the online dating route at his age, but he had to do something because he was becoming aware of his own darkness, and he didn't like it!

ARRIVING HOME

Simon arrived home extremely late at night, due to booking a late flight. When Debs heard his key in the lock, she was surprised that he'd returned because some part of her thought he might stay on in France for a few more weeks! She turned over in bed and pretended to be sleeping, then cautiously opened one eye as he came through the bedroom door and slid into bed next to her. The next thing she knew was that he was hugged up to her back, with his mouth resting on the back of her neck. She didn't move, still pretending she was asleep. After spending time with Stewie for the last fortnight, she was confused especially when, a few evenings ago, after a trip to Weston, they both put the children to bed together and ended up having a long hug and kiss. Debs didn't want to be unfaithful to Simon. The situation was crazy, imagine wanting to be unfaithful with her husband! She'd come to realise that she should have spent time on her own and not jumped in so quickly with Simon. But then, she was pregnant.

'Debs, are you asleep? I've missed you. The retreat was great though, plus Sapphire was there, which was good. She came for a past life regression, it was fascinating! I expect she'll tell you about it. How've you been?'

'Yeah, OK, Simon. I'm tired. I've been doing a lot with the children, taking them all over the place.'

'OK, Debs, I get it. We can talk in the morning, but I've missed you,' whispered Simon as he moved closer to her and slid his hand along her thigh.

'I'm asleep,' she replied.

Her sexual desire for this man, even after not seeing him for several weeks, had taken a dive. He rolled over and faced the other way. At least he's got the message, she thought. But she didn't doubt that he would continue what he had started in the morning, because Simon continually desired sex, and Debs was usually happy to oblige. Yet while Simon was away, all she could see was the vision of her and Stewie kissing, and she was shocked that she wanted more.

The next day, Debs was up and out of bed before Simon woke, making the girls breakfast. They were full of 'what are we doing today?' and 'when can we go to the beach again?' because they had such a brilliant time in Weston. Debs managed to calm them by saying, not today because Simon was home, and they might go out for a picnic tea later, which quietened them a little. She opened the door to the garden to let in some air.

Simon then appeared in the kitchen. He still looked tired but had put on a T-shirt and shorts and walked straight out into the garden barefoot to get some sun. The girls ran out to him, all wanting hugs and kisses. He pulled Jessica up onto his lap; she was definitely a Daddy's girl. It was always, 'Daddy, Daddy, where's Daddy?' and Simon looked happy to be back with his daughters. He kissed and hugged Florence and Elsbeth from his garden chair, and all three of them were hanging on to him. Debs heard him say, 'Steady, you'll have me over,' but he was laughing. The girls then ran into the kitchen to eat their breakfast, full of excitement.

Debs walked out into the sun and sat in a fold-up chair next to Simon. 'We've had brilliant weather. We went to the beach with Stewie last week, it was fun. He's like his old self again. It was good for the girls to see their dad.'

'And what about you, did you enjoy it? Because life isn't always about children.'

'You say that, Simon, but I always look at the holidays as their time. They find school and nursery tiring, and it's also good for Jessica to spend time with her sisters instead of being with her childminder because they entertain her.'

'Are you planning any more trips with Stewie?'

'I don't know. He's quite busy with clients now. It's nice for him to see the girls when he hasn't seen them for so long. He says they've really changed, which they have.'

'I'm going away on another retreat in a few weeks, but it's only for a week. In the meantime, I've got to catch up with my therapy clients because I have loads of emails to answer. I thought I'd make the most of the sun this morning and get on with my emails and scheduling appointments this afternoon, because it looks like rain later.'

'Oh, that's a shame on your first day home. I told the girls we could go out for a picnic or something.'

'Well, Debs, it's OK to make plans for us, but please ask me first and check the weather, or we'll have a soggy picnic.'

'If you say so, Simon. I can't believe that you've just come home and you're already being a killjoy. I should have asked Stewie instead.'

'Do what you want, Debs. You're a free spirit, the same as me, and we have an open relationship.'

'Open relationship? No, we don't. We're a couple with a child. An open relationship is something entirely different. How was France? I discovered Sapphire was there too after you'd left, no one told me she was going.'

'Do you have a problem with Sapphire? She's your mother-in-law, Debs, so I'm hardly likely to go there, am I? Besides, we're friends—always have been, always will be. We have an incredible link from a past life.'

'I thought you said that you and I were together in a past life?'

'We were. You, Stewie, and I were in a karmic love triangle, which is still playing out in this life and Sapphire was my daughter. I guess that's why she looks up to me in this life, and why I feel so protective of her. After Stewie left the tribe, I was made chief, and I married you. When we married, you were already carrying our daughter.'

'That sounds too incredible to be true. I think I'll get myself a coffee and tell the kids it's going to rain, so we won't be going for a picnic today. If the weather looks up, I'll take them on my own tomorrow, or you can come if you have time.'

'I'll see what I can do. I have three clients booked in tomorrow. They're regulars, but I might be able to finish at four and join you then.'

Debs walked back into the kitchen. The sun was hot, and she realised suntan lotion was a good idea if she was going to sit outside because her skin was quite sensitive. It didn't appear that Simon was going to put himself out for the remaining weeks of the summer holidays. She'd have to accept it, in the same way she'd accepted Stewie's unusual working habits, but for some reason, she thought Simon would spend more time with her because his therapy work would allow him more flexibility. But it appeared that any time off he had was based purely around what he wanted to do.

One thing was for sure: if Simon wasn't going to give any of his precious time to their family, she could always ask Stewie. What had she got to lose? Once again, the image of them kissing came over her, sending tingles through her body. This was crazy. None of it made sense, particularly the past life stuff. Simon obviously believed it was true; she'd never seen him so ignited by something. But how did she know he wasn't making the whole thing up?

He's doing my head in, she thought, and he's been back less than a day.

She'd ask him to mind the children in the garden while she walked to the local shops to stock up a bit. She'd look in a few charity shops for some clothes while she was at it. The free-spirited kind, which would attract a man who had been given a second chance!

ROUTINE

Debs and Simon settled back into a routine, and although Simon managed to find the time for a few family outings, which pleased Debs, she had begun to find his need for independence irritating. He constantly talked about where he wanted to go, as if he was still single. Jessica loved having her daddy at home, and Simon sometimes took her off in his car, which Debs found anti-social of him. They were a family or at least she thought so, and it left the other two constantly asking where their sister was. In addition, if she had domestic stuff to do, the older girls easily became bored, and their sister was out being spoilt by her dad. In the end, Debs decided to say something to Simon about it. Jessica had fallen asleep, and the girls had gone to a friend's house for the afternoon, which was rare!

'I know you want to spend time with Jessica but taking her out on her own makes the other two jealous, and it looks like she's your favourite.'

'Well, she is. And although I love Elsbeth and Florence, they are yours and Stewie's children. Sometimes it's nice to give Jessica a bit of one-to-one. I was thinking of taking her to see my parents next week before I go on the retreat.'

'I thought we were all going to Devon to meet your parents as a family.'

'We were, but I want to sleep over and spend some proper time with them, and they can't put all of us up. I phoned Mum this morning, and she said that I could go next week. I thought I'd take a couple of days off work.'

'You told me yesterday that you had loads of clients, and you've only just come back from France. What a shame. I was really looking forward to meeting them. Besides, this coming weekend, Sapphire's asked us over for a meal. John is coming down from Scotland, and we're all invited.'

'Will Stewie be there?' asked Simon.

'Of course, Stewie will be there. He lives there! She's going to do a BBQ in the garden and include everyone. It will be great for the kids to see us all together, and they haven't seen their grandfather since God knows when. I think since he went to live in Scotland. He hasn't even met Jessica. Look, you don't have to come if you don't want to. Go to your mum's, but I thought, as you were friends with Sapphire, you'd want to come.'

'OK, I'll be there. I can visit my parents on Monday. The girls are going back to school next week, so there shouldn't be this jealousy problem, but you'll have to let the childminder know we'll be gone for a few days. Mum keeps asking about Jessica, and I owe it to them to take her now. She's three years old.'

'Yes, I'll let her know. That's not a problem as long as you can fit it in your busy schedule. I guess I can meet them another time. I do have a lot on with the girls going back to school and loads to prepare before I return. I felt it would have been nice to be included.'

'Debs, are you going to be able to cope with my free-spirited ways? I do care about you, but I need to be able to do my own thing.'

'You care about me?'

'Yes, you know I care about you,' replied Simon.

'But you don't love me?'

'Love is complex!'

'No, it isn't. You either love someone, or you don't,' replied Debs, who was feeling angry.

'There are many types of love. My love for you goes a long way back, and I'm committed to looking after you.'

'Really? It doesn't feel that way. It feels like you're fulfilling some sort of boring obligation.'

'Debs, you're not boring. It's just that you have to respect someone's need for freedom, otherwise it feels smothering and controlling.'

'Is it so wrong to want someone around for me and the children? A person who loves spending time and holidays with us, rather than wanting to go on holiday on their own? What I need in my life is support.'

'You have my support, Debs. You also had it while I was away in France, and you'll have it when I'm at my parents.' I don't have to be sitting in front of you to support you. What you want is co-dependence, and I'm not that person.'

'So, you're supporting me from your mobile with emojis and texts?'

'Debs, you know I would be there if there was a real problem.'

'That's not the point though, is it, Simon?'

'I go to the park with the children, and I receive a text to say that you've already left for France. That's hardly fair, is it, to leave me doing everything?'

'I said I'd come with you to the BBQ on Sunday. I'm only going to see my parents for a couple of days. I'm sorry I left so quickly for France without talking it through, but as I already explained, Lara desperately needed my help, so I had to get there early to help set up the gazebos.'

'Stewie said they were already up!'

'Stewie? What does he know about it? Was he there? Honestly, Debs, you are blowing things out of proportion. You're looking for an argument over nothing. I tried several times to call you from France, but you didn't answer.'

'I don't know if I can do this, Simon. I don't like not knowing where you are or what you're up to.'

'You don't trust me?'

'I did, but now I've found out that you're only 'fond' of me, things feel different.'

'We have a good relationship, Debs. Please don't ruin it with unrealistic expectations. We agreed to be together because of Jessica, and we have a strong connection, but I have many strong connections.

There's no need to be jealous because I'm not going to go off with anyone else. I'm committed to this family. I'm staying.'

Debs started to cry. She didn't know what she wanted. She thought she wanted Simon, but since Stewie had come back into her life—and he'd changed so much—she was no longer sure about anything. Her world had become a confusing place.

'That's a great dress, Debs. You look pretty hot,' remarked Simon, trying to change the subject. 'The girls are both out, aren't they, and Jessica's asleep, so let's run upstairs quickly.'

'I don't think so, Simon. I'm feeling numb right now.'

'Stewie got to you, has he? Did he give the girls that dream catcher hanging in their room? You know it's exactly the same colours as the one I have in my therapy room.'

'I know. I told him that.'

'Interesting,' whispered Simon.

'No, not really. It's just a dream catcher from the crystal shop in town—there are loads of them. Why do you always have to make something out of things, search for the hidden meaning? Don't you realise how annoying that is? All of this 'you and Stewie had a life as brothers' is absolute rubbish. You seem far more interested in this past lives stuff than in what I've been doing. You didn't even ask what I did while you were away.'

'I'm sorry, Debs. What did you do?'

'Stewie and I took the children to Weston-Super-Mare, and they loved it.'

'OK, sounds fun. That was good of him. I must thank him for taking Jessica out when I see him on Sunday. Now, can we please stop talking about this? I don't have a problem with you not wanting sex, but I do have a problem with us arguing. Isn't it time to pick up the girls from their friends'?'

Debs looked at the kitchen clock and went to fetch her car keys. This afternoon had gone so quickly, and neither of them had got anything done. If Jessica woke up crying, like she often did when she couldn't see anyone in the room with her, then Simon would have to go to her, after all, he was only working in the garden! As Debs took the road to the Stevens' house, part of her felt completely detached. She guessed she was in shock. She and Simon had been together for four years, and he didn't love her? 'Fond of' was an expression you used for a pet, or an acquaintance. Was he for real? When would someone genuinely love her for who she was? What the hell did she have to do? Other people had loving relationships. The Stevens certainly did. So why did she always feel like there was something missing?

SUNDAY BBQ

Sapphire was in her element, buzzing around getting everything ready for the family BBQ. John had agreed to take care of the cooking because he enjoyed cooking outside, which was a relief to her as she had enough on her plate! Various salads had been laid out in the kitchen for people to help themselves. There were some great desserts, a pavlova, a huge chocolate gateau and a couple of cheesecakes. Sapphire was convinced that they had everything covered and it was now time to relax a bit!

Stewie was sitting by the pool in denim shorts and a bright green luminous T-shirt. He didn't usually wear bright colours, and couldn't imagine what had happened to him lately, because he really loved them now. They lifted his mood. He'd made a simple bar in the dining room and had wine, beers, and soft drinks. He wiped the dust off the glasses, which hadn't been used for months, then decided that it would be better to just sit back and let Sapphire and John get on with it. He heard Debs, Simon and the children arrive, the girls tore down the side of the pool towards him, apart from Jessica who was holding her daddy's hand. 'Slow down, you're not allowed to run next to the pool. 'You know that' shouted Stewie.

'Elsbeth, Florence, play on the climbing frame next to the cabin and get rid of some of that energy. I'll give you a shout when the food's ready,' Debs said a little more gently because Stewie sounded harsh!

Stewie stood up and walked over to Debs and Simon to say hello. His heart sank when he saw them together. Simon looked so young, from what he understood, he was forty-two, but he certainly didn't look it. 'Hi, you two, how are things going? We're lucky to have picked such a nice day. Can I fetch you both a drink?'

'Yes please, we're getting a taxi home later, so we can enjoy ourselves. I'll have a lager, or light beer if you have one, and do you want white Debs?' asked Simon.

Debs looked at Stewie, what a bright colour green T-shirt, another change she thought; it's almost luminous.

'Yes, white wine please,' she said, taking her eyes away from the T-shirt .'

'Yeah, it's bright, not my usual colour is it? Sapphire thought it was a good idea, *helps the heart chakra rebalance* or something! I'll get the drinks.'

Simon went to take a seat and then decided to say hello to John.'

'Hi John, how's Scotland? I bet the golf's good.'

'Yes, everything's good there to be honest, I love it, but I do miss the family. I've reverted to the occasional whisky now and again, so it might be an idea for me to book in a session with you while I'm here. Last time you worked on me, it tasted like cat's piss, which wasn't ideal, but at least it stopped me drinking it for a while.'

'Cat's piss, how interesting! I don't think anyone's said that! You'd likely benefit from a few more sessions John. Anyway, nice to see you and thanks for inviting me today. I'm vegetarian like Sapphire, so I'll stick to veggie burgers and sausages, and leave the meat to you and Stewie. Where did Sapphire go?'

'Oh, she's in the kitchen. Her mobile went off. No doubt she's talking to the secret man she met in France.

'Really I wasn't aware of that, but if she's on the phone, I won't interrupt her.'

Sapphire was talking to Tom Bear, who had called her regularly since she returned from France.

'I'm busy today, Tom, I have the whole family here, so I can't talk for long, but I've left Stewie and John in charge, salads and desserts are my forte.'

'How's John? Are you two getting along all right?'

'Yes, he's all right, he's helpful. He was really excited about seeing the grandkids, he really missed them, but it sounds like he loves living in Scotland. He's met someone too, although they're just friends for now, I may have told you about it.'

'Okay, I'll let you go. It sounds like you're going to be busy. I'd love us to spend some time together, but I'll call or text in the week and we can sort something out!'

'I'd love that,' replied Sapphire.

John walked into the kitchen. Have you got a large plate for me to put some of this food on, or something with a lid to keep it warm? Sorry to interrupt, were you on the phone to your French lover?'

'He isn't a French lover; he's a doctor from Bath, actually.'

'A doctor, wow that's a surprise, I would have thought you would have gone for someone more unconventional.'

'He is, he used to be a doctor, but he now practices first aid, yoga and that sort of thing. He's retired.'

'Retired, I wish I could do that. Anyway, can you please pass me something for the food, or it will be burning. I doubt Stewie will rescue it because he's not doing much by the look of things.'

'I think he's the barman, I've seen him getting drinks.'

'Ok, are you coming out, to be with our guests,'

'Yes, I'm coming, but go on ahead because I want to get some plates out,' replied Sapphire.

John was curious about Sapphire's mystery man. He couldn't imagine her with another doctor. He didn't want to press her too much because it was her business, but part of him was still hankering after the old Susan, as it appeared unlikely that things were going to work out with Sushan. He smiled. Everything felt ironic. He had to admit there were *coincidences or synchronicities* as Sapphire would say, that seemed unbelievable, but he wasn't going to start believing in her mumbo jumbo in order to pull her back. After returning home on Friday, he quickly realised that Sapphire was very settled here, and it was doubtful that she'd be willing to start a new life in Scotland. He loved it there, and despite missing the family he felt it unlikely that he'd uproot again to move back to Bristol.

Stewie, Debs and Simon were all sitting around the BBQ and the girls were happily playing a ball game at the end of the garden.

'I'll sort the children's food out first,' suggested Debs.

'No, that's ok, you relax. I'll do that,' replied Sapphire, who produced three small plates loaded with salad and was rapidly adding sausages and burgers. 'I'll take these to the kids and then we can have a proper chat.'

'A proper chat isn't that dangerous?' joked John, who had started a second beer.

'How's Florence getting on at school?' asked Sapphire when she returned.

'We don't want to talk about that Susan. We want to know what happened in France?' asked John.

'For goodness sake, can you please stop calling me that. It's not a term of endearment to call someone by the wrong name. I'm Sapphire, please get it right, don't slip back into old habits! Moving on, many things happened in France. I had a past life regression with Simon, which was very revealing, and I also met a man called Tom Jones who has become a good friend.'

'Tom Jones, as in 'the Tom Jones?' asked Debs.

'No, of course not, that would be crazy! He's called White Bear; well, that's his Shamanic name, but I decided to call him Tom Bear because I felt more comfortable with that.'

'White Bear wasn't he the other twin I mentioned in the regression?' replied Simon.

'What! Please don't start down that path again,' replied Debs.

'What do you mean by that?' replied Simon.

'You know exactly what I mean, *trying to make things fit*. So, you have some Native American fantasy, and the name White Bear popped into your head, then by sheer chance you meet a man with that name and assume it's connected to him. What utter rubbish and on that note, I'm going to see if the kids are all right,' replied an exasperated Debs.

'I agree with Debs, I think this making things fit can get a bit out of hand. I thought my friend in Scotland was called Susan, then she told me that her name is the Chinese version, which is pronounced differently, it's Sushan! When I heard them say her name at the surgery, it sounded like Susan. *It's so easy to make assumptions to try and make the pieces fit*. We hear what we want to hear, depending on our *psychological state*,' explained John.

'*Emotional state*,' replied Sapphire, then smiled. 'Did you say Sushan is an acupuncturist, how interesting? Have you tried it for your back?'

'No, not yet, but I'm going to when I get back, as the drive from Scotland has taken its toll. She has great results and is always booked, which is good for the surgery.'

'She sounds amazing, and she lives near you? Yes, in the same village, we go birdwatching together, she absolutely loves it.'

'How convenient,' Sapphire replied, then realised that she may have sounded a little sarcastic, which wasn't her intention, but she didn't really know what to say. She was bored and wished that she'd invited John Bear. Stewie looked awkward around Simon, and Debs had stayed at the end of the garden with the children to avoid any more past life regression conflict with Simon!'

'Desserts anyone,' she shouted as she noticed the children running towards her!

'I want strawberry,' shouted Jessica.

'There's plenty of strawberries,' insisted Sapphire, who was trying to keep everyone calm. Debs stepped up and put Jessica on her lap with a strawberry while the other two helped themselves to everything!'

'Look at those red curls, she looks like a little treasure, and I hear she likes the doctor's kit,' John remarked.

'Well, someone had to, didn't they?' replied Stewie with a grin.

'I hear that you're getting on extremely well with your counselling clients, Stewie. Great career change. I admire you for that, and you're already busy, amazing!'

'Yes, I'm busy. I wish I'd done this twenty years ago. I feel as if I'm a much better person than I was before, and I love helping people. Fortunately, Sapphire is happy to share her space with me, which is kind of her because she is precious about her cabin.'

'Yes, I remember that well. I'm still waiting for my porridge, but I don't think I'm likely to find my place back at the table, now that she's met Big Bear,'

'White Bear,' Simon said, correcting him. He'd started to think that John had drunk one beer too many, because he obviously felt sorry for himself.

'Can you please give up talking about my recent friendship? It's more important to me that I've met someone who I like, than what he's called! I'm a free spirit like Simon, and I'm going to encounter many people on my path now I teach yoga.'

'So have you got any more trips coming up, where you can teach?' asked John.'

'I might be going to one with a friend at the end of the month, and we will do the class together, if I can fit the retreat in around my clients.'

Jessica suddenly started screaming at the top of her voice and Debs hurriedly carried her across the garden to run her arm under the tap. 'I think she's been stung by a wasp, or something. I can't see the sting, but her arm is swelling up. I need to take her home because she looks tired. I'll call the taxi and leave now, if you don't mind, but I don't want to be rude.'

'I'll take her home,' replied Simon. I've only had one small beer, so I should be fine to drive. I'll pick you up in the morning Debs if you want to stay over.'

'Yes ok, thanks Simon, that's great of you to offer.'

Simon carried Jessica to the car and put her in her car seat. He felt relieved to be leaving because the conversation felt awkward with John, who seemed to have fallen into victim mode. He'd contact him tomorrow and ask if he wanted to book in a few hypnotherapy appointments while he was down, although he had the feeling that he'd be going back to Scotland soon, if Sapphire's man was mentioned again! When they got home, he'd put some wasp ointment on Jessica's arm, and then they could snuggle up and watch a film together, before she went to bed. As soon as he got through the door, he noticed a text from Debs to say, 'really sorry you had to go Simon, I hope you'll be alright on your own with Jessica.' He didn't know how to reply, she was doing it again. Why couldn't she just leave him alone? They were fine, so he replied, 'all good, we'll see you in the morning.'

As soon as Simon had left, Stewie moved his chair closer to Debs, so they could talk to each other.

'How do you feel about Simon doing all these retreats?' Stewie asked.

'Not that great to be honest. He's not going to change, in fact he's taking Jessica to his parents in Devon tomorrow, they've never met her and she's already three years old, it's crazy. We were going as a family, but we'll do that another time besides the girls will be back at school.'

'I find him to be a little dismissive to be honest, and if you have to put up with that, it's hardly surprising you're upset. I've decided to step up with Elsbeth and Florence, I'll bring them over here more often, as well as taking them out. You're welcome to come too, especially if Simon's away, and you can also bring Jessica, two or three of them, it makes no odds to me.'

'Thanks Stewie, Simon said, that I want co-dependency, and he could never be in a relationship like that, and he can support me from afar! I wouldn't say that I entirely agree with him, as it's all right for him to say that, when I'm the one left doing all the work, while he's away having fun! Anyway, I'm going to get another glass of wine. Sapphire said we could stay over, which means I can relax a little now. Debs walked into the dining room and Stewie followed her. As she reached for a glass, he suddenly said, 'I'll pour you one because I know, which is which, I'm the barman.'

'Oh really, and does the barman have any special secrets?'

'Only this,' he said taking Debs in his arms.

'Sapphire will see us, or the kids, honestly Stewie, we can't cuddle in here.'

'Why not, I'm your husband?' Stewie said indignantly.

'I feel so confused, lately, I was sure Simon was the one for me, my soul mate, but I'm even wrong about that. He has many soulmates, and he said he was fond of me, but that isn't love.'

'That doesn't surprise me, because a man who's that wrapped up in himself doesn't have any spare energy to love another, does he?'

'So, you knew?'

'No, I didn't know that he was just fond of you, but you needed someone in your life after what we went through, and having another child on your own would have been difficult. He obviously has a problem with commitment. What we had was special in the early days, and we both loved each other.'

'He isn't leaving me; he's just going to do his own thing.'

'Well, the choice is yours. You know how I feel about you. Mum is heading this way, so let's go out and see if the girls are all right because they'll start to get bored.'

'I'll think about what you said, he's off on another retreat soon, so we'll have time to talk more about it then.'

'Hi, you two, what are you doing hiding in here? It's like heaven outside, the sun is so beautiful. The girls are getting tired though. They can go up to their room anytime you like, if you want to take them up.'

'We were just getting drinks,' replied Stewie, but he knew Sapphire thought there was more going on than that.

'If you two want to clear up, I'll put the children to bed, then you can finish chatting.'

'Really, that sounds like a good idea,' replied Debs. Where's John gone?'

'To his usual haunt, the conservatory. I heard him snoring. Can you believe he'd do that this early in the evening.'

'Does Big Bear snore?' asked Stewie.

'I don't know, and he isn't called Big Bear, he's the one from Goldilocks who didn't get his porridge,' replied Sapphire forcing a smile!

'Ah, he didn't get his oats?' replied Stewie.

'Right, you two have had too much to drink, so I'm getting the girls now before they get any more excited and putting them to bed! Hopefully, you can manage to clear up!'

Debs erupted with laughter. 'Stewie, you shouldn't have said that. It was rude.'

'I know, but it was funny though. There's John permanently waiting for his big bowl of porridge, which he never gets and along comes Big Bear.'

'I think he's called White Bear, but near enough!'

'Poor Sapphire, I think all these bear jokes have got out of hand. I bet she wishes she hadn't mentioned it. Tom Jones would have been taken more seriously. Where do these plates go?' Debs asked.'

'Over here, what great teamwork. Hopefully, we'll get this done quickly, and we can have coffee in the peace of the garden. I think Sapphire will be hours with the girls, reading them stories, and I can hear John snoring!'

'Do you think he'll stay on a bit?' asked Debs.

'No, I don't think so. I bet he gets up early tomorrow and drives back to Scotland. He's feeling a little disillusioned about Sapphire moving on. John always hoped that Sapphire would come round to his way of thinking, or at least meet him halfway, which is naive because *there must be a time when you accept that you've grown apart and it isn't anyone's fault*. People change, that's all there is to it. Unless both of you agree to go into therapy, that's where I come in, but as you know I had to go through some drastic realisations first and John isn't at that stage yet. However, having another relationship may force him to.'

SAYING GOODBYE

Sapphire awoke to the sound of John packing, and she hurriedly put on her dressing gown to make herself a cup of tea. It was only seven, and it felt early after last night's BBQ. Why didn't he say something last night. He could have disappeared while she was still in bed!

'John, what are you doing? It's so early!'

'Yes, but it's an exceedingly long trip and I might take a break or two, so I need to get off soon. I have surgery tomorrow, and I don't want to be home too late tonight.'

'I hope you enjoyed seeing the family yesterday. I'm sad that you're leaving so soon because it was nice having you here.'

'I had great fun Sapphire, but needs must. Sushan has just text and we might meet for a quick drink later, believe it or not, she said that she missed me this weekend!'

'Well, that's great, isn't it?'

'I must let go of the past and move on. It was nice being here, but it brought up old memories, so it was difficult at times. I'm glad Stewie's sorted himself out at last. He's looking good!'

'Yes, he's dong well. Have trip John and please let me know you've arrived home safely. Stay in touch.'

'Of course I will, and I hope it goes well with Great Bear,'

Sapphire looked at him in disbelief! Did John have a problem remembering names?

'And Sushan, you can bring her with you next time if you like.'

John suddenly gave her a kiss on the cheek and opened the front door. 'I'll keep the key because I still own the house,'

Sapphire was going to say, half the house, but then decided not to. They would have to sort this out sometime in the future, and it wasn't going to be easy! She smiled at him, then said, 'Goodbye, drive carefully,' and he left.

It surprised Sapphire how empty the house felt after John had left. She was relieved to hear Stewie getting up, and no doubt Debs and the girls would soon be wanting breakfast. It was a nice idea to have the BBQ, but she wasn't sure if it was wise, to have Simon and Stewie together. Was something going on between Stewie and Debs. Had they been kissing? She felt as if she interrupted something in the dining room yesterday, and her intuition was usually right!

Debs walked downstairs with the girls followed by Stewie; they looked like a family. They sorted out the girls' breakfast and then Debs walked out into the garden with Sapphire.

'I've been thinking I might ask Simon to leave. He wants to travel and do his own thing, so he can! He can visit Jessica whenever he wants, take her to his parents for the holidays. He doesn't want to do things as a couple; besides, I've realised since he went away to France, that I'm still in love with Stewie. I know he was unfaithful to me in the past. It was a terrible thing, him having an affair with Georgia, and going to prison, but I forgave him months ago. He's a different person now, and I think he'll stand by me. Do you think I'm a terrible person?' asked Debs.

'It doesn't matter what I think, does it? Why would you be a terrible person if Simon isn't there half the time, and he's not in love with you? Let him move on,' replied Sapphire.

Yeah, I don't want him to feel like I'm an obligation, or to favour Jessica in front of Elsbeth and Florence!'

'Debs, sometimes it's time to stop worrying about others and start looking after yourself. There comes a time when we need to move into self-love. When we do that, we allow others to love us, and people-pleasing becomes a thing of the past. It isn't that you wouldn't help someone if they needed it, just that it's time to stand in your own power and create healthy boundaries. You deserve the best, not someone who is merely fond of you, but a person who loves you for the wonderful person you are.'

'So, you knew Simon wasn't in love with me?'

'No, but I know Simon, and you might be surprised to hear, and I'm telling you this in the strictest confidence, that he has other children too, twins. They run in his family, so you're lucky.'

'Jessica has half brothers or sisters out there that she hasn't met?'

'He was going to marry Sarah, but he didn't want to take on the twins because he has a problem with responsibility. Like I told you, like him or not, Simon's a free spirit.'

'I think I'm going to focus on that,'

'Focus on what?' asked Sapphire.

'Being a free spirit,' Debs replied.

'I think that's an excellent idea!' replied Sapphire, who thought Debs had never looked so radiant!

www.ingramcontent.com/pod-product-compliance
Lightning Source LLC
LaVergne TN
LVHW051625080426
835511LV00016B/2188